MW00569617

Free to Be

FREE TO BE

DEFEATING
INSECURITY

TRANSFORMING
RELATIONSHIPS

BUILDING
CHARACTER

SARAH TUN

Essence PUBLISHING

Belleville, Ontario, Canada

Free to Be: Defeating Insecurity,
Transforming Relationships, Building Character
Copyright © 2012, Sarah Tun

*All Rights Reserved. No part of this publication may be reproduced, stored in
a retrieval system or transmitted in any form or by any means—electronic,
mechanical, photocopy, recording or any other—except for brief quotations
in printed reviews, without the prior permission of the author.*

All Scripture quotations, unless otherwise specified, are from *The Holy Bible,
New King James Version.* Copyright © 1979 Thomas Nelson Inc., Publishers.
• Scripture quotations marked KJV are from *The Holy Bible, King James
Version (Authorised Version),* Copyright © 1958, The National Publishing Co.,
Philadephia, PA. RSV are from the *Revised Standard Version* of the Bible,
copyright © 1952, 1971, CollinsBible, a division of HarperCollins Publishers,
Glasgow, and are used by permission. All rights reserved.

ISBN: 978-1-55452-731-1
LSI Edition: 978-1-55452-732-8
E-book ISBN: 978-1-55452-733-5

Cataloguing data available from Library and Archives Canada

To order additional copies, visit:
www.essencebookstore.com

For more information, please contact:
freetobewrite@hotmail.com or sarahtunexaminelife.blogspot.com

Attention churches, small groups and Christian Unions:
Quantity discounts are available on bulk purchases for educational study or
gift purposes. Book excerpts can be created to fit specific needs.

For information: Contact Sarah Tun, Box 72, Bath, Ontario K0H 1G0
or contact via email/blog as above.

Essence Publishing is a Christian Book Publisher dedicated to
furthering the work of Christ through the written word.
For more information, contact:

20 Hanna Court, Belleville, Ontario, Canada K8P 5J2.
Phone: 1-800-238-6376. Fax: (613) 962-3055.
Email: info@essence-publishing.com
Web site: www.essence-publishing.com

Dedication

The book is dedicated to all those who desire to face and overcome their fears. And to Pastor Cynthia Stith who first engaged me to believe the Lord always keeps His promises.

Acknowledgments

I would like to thank my family and my Lord without whom I would not have had the challenges to face nor the opportunities to grow. Thank you to David Heron, Rob Lacey, Julie Anderson, Rob Parsons, Michael Ross-Watson, Sarah Pianarosa, Anna Tun, Mark Kotchapaw, Bill Duffy, Erin McCormick and James Hunt. At various stages you engaged with me in the birthing of this book to publication. Thanks to Terry Harris who introduced me to Essence Publishing and to those at Essence, in particular Sherrill Brunton and Timothy Fransky, for their encouragement, experience, and advice. Finally, thank you to my husband Alan, my mentor, friend and love, for his wisdom, patience and support. May God always be at the centre of our lives and of our marriage.

Table of Contents

SECTION IV

Becoming Free: Applying Scripture to the Healing Process

SECTION V

Staying Free: Maintaining Security, Growing in Character

Preface

Peace in this fast-paced and competitive world is desirable but rare. There are different kinds of peace—peace from war, peace with neighbours, internal peace. The type of peace I refer to is peace of mind, which is anxiety's opposite. To be free from worry is to have peace.

What causes worry? Finances, concern for others' well-being, a lack of control over our circumstances—all of these trigger worry. This book focuses on insecurity, the anxiety that springs from the fear that we aren't accepted. We worry about our relationships if we don't feel loved. Unconditional love is the only solution to insecurity.

So where do we find unconditional love? And how do we sustain it?

This book is about you and me and how to overcome the nagging doubts about ourselves and our relationships. To be free from hiding behind a false persona and to find total peace of mind is what we want. That is the secure life. Anything less falls short.

Friends, it is liberating to live emotionally and socially *secure,* to feel loved unconditionally and to express freely who we were born to be. When we are free to be who we were created to be, then we are ready to do what we were created to do.

I fought insecurity and won. I believe if I can, anyone can, which is why I've written this book. Through my journey, I have come to long for others to the find the same peace that I have found.

Do you experience lasting peace? Do you feel loved beyond measure and confident that love is unshakable? How wonderful to have such security! If you've got that, I believe you are rare indeed. This book is a prescription to get to and remain in that state, regardless of your circumstances.

Do you know that we were created and are meant to live in security, confident we are loved for who we are? It took me half a lifetime to realize this truth. I believe we were created to love and to be loved simply for who we are. There are different kinds of love: romantic, sexual, brotherly. But the love I am referring to is unconditional love, love that is based on our existence, rather than on what we do in our existence. And when we experience this pure love, we experience pure freedom too.

Many of us have unwittingly settled for less than the personal freedom intended for us. We endure insecurity, fearing we will make a mistake and bring rejection upon ourselves, because we don't know anything else. From the cradle our greatest need has been love, and perhaps we have grown sensitive to rejection.

I didn't recognize the full extent of my insecurity until my thirties. I wasted many years being anxious and stressed about my relationships because I thought it was normal. But it isn't. While conflict in life is unavoidable, insecurity is a learned response, and what has been learned can be unlearned. I'd like you to glimpse my insecurity and my journey to overcome it, so that you can identify yours and be encouraged also.

When I learned that peace was possible, I then became aware that I didn't have it. Only then did I begin the long but rewarding road to healing. Now that I've overcome anxiety and found the peace that comes with self-acceptance, I long for others to find the same, so that all of us can be who we were created to be.

Insecure: by definition means "unsafe," "liable to give way" (*The Concise Oxford Dictionary of Current English*); "not secure," "not confident of safety," "not sufficiently strong or guarded" (*The New Webster Encyclopedic Dictionary of the English Language*).

I lived most of my early life with a strong sense of self-doubt and uncertainty when it came to my personal relationships. Though I was an able student and popular within my circle and later a competent professional in my field who was respected by my colleagues, I always felt isolated and unlovable. I thought I was trapped, wanting to please everyone but unable, and therefore unable to be accepted by everyone. I have since transformed my thinking, and so I am no longer riddled with anxiety and fear.

"The mass of men lead lives of quiet desperation."[1] I don't believe that we are designed to be uneasy in our relationships, but we look for love in the wrong places, and therefore, so often, we end up protecting our wounded hearts. I offer an overview of my experience, combining Scriptures and suggestions to guide you on your way to freedom. Having analyzed my circumstances, I offer the practical direction I took so that, like me, you will be enabled to overcome the nagging feelings of inadequacy and fear that I did. To replace negativity with inner acceptance releases us into wholeness.

During my journey from a sort of shadowy existence to a life of what feels like sparkling assurance, I discovered truths and tools that I want to share. None of us will be accepted by everybody we meet. But we don't have to fear rejection, even when exposed to other's disdain. Because fear saps our confidence and steals our freedom, we need to learn how to rise above rejection.

---

1 Henry David Thoreau, *Walden*, 1854, http://en.wikiquote.org/wiki/Henry_David_Thoreau.

The first step to discovering freedom is to recognize that change is not effected by an act of will but by a surrendering of it. It is *"not by might"* but by the power of the Spirit of God (Zechariah 4:6).

The Bible says, *"Learn to do good; Seek justice,* **Rebuke the oppressor;** *Defend the fatherless, Plead for the widow."*[2] When I discovered this quote, I was smitten by it. God tells us that oppression will come but it can be overcome. How to *correct* the *oppression* that lies *within us* is the course this book offers. Believe! It is possible to live free from fear—from the worry, panic and anxiety of approval seeking. My prayer and hope is that each of us who takes this journey to security will become *the entire* person she or he was created to be.

---

[2] Isaiah 1:17, emphasis added.

Section I

Acknowledging the Problem
A Bit of My Story

This is a book for brave-hearted souls who want to face and overcome fear and live in personal freedom. To overcome insecurity we need to grip truth and hang on to it. We start by looking in the mirror and recognizing that the person reflected back has both positive *and* negative qualities, and that is normal. For some it will be easier to see what is good. For me it was easier to recognize my shortcomings.

Was I Born Tied Up in Knots?

The success story that unfolds begins necessarily with who I was before I found security. I praise God that He led me in a gentle and consistent way that taught me about His love and His power in my life. But in order to find His way, I first had to travel a lonely journey.

Turmoil existed within me sometime after age five. I remember being bold and assertive in kindergarten. But sometime afterward, a fear of rejection began to take hold. I was expressive and affectionate but had non-demonstrative parents and was the object of bullying as a child in school. I believe these were contributing factors to my decline in confidence.

For almost as long as I can remember, I felt unaccepted, so I lived in pursuit of the acceptance I lacked. As a child and young adult, I often felt excluded and was sensitive to being sidelined. My insecurity did not end with education, employment or even marriage. Into adulthood, one-to-one conversations with friends would often shift to me as the subject as I sought approval. I sought affirmation for my decisions and my identity. Like most teens, I was full of self-doubt, but this phase did not end after adolescence. It extended into my thirties.

Integrity has always been a part of me, and instinctively I knew that to be authentic was preferable to being phony, but I felt anxious whether alone or in company, whether I hid my vulnerability or was sincere. My anxiety went deeper than recognizing that I should try to be nice so people would like me. I believed that my personality was flawed and unworthy of affirmation. I needed encouragement, attention and love. But my existence was full of self-recrimination, so I isolated myself from the love and encouragement I needed by hiding when I felt vulnerable and putting on a cloak of self-sufficiency when I felt strong.

By adulthood I was trapped. Rejecting myself and hiding behind a false persona, I would never find satisfying acceptance for who I was. Yet the alternative, to be authentic and risk being rejected by others, was unimaginable. Frustrated and fearful, I did not like to expose my heart. Although others regarded me as confident, capable and courageous, I only felt stressed, anxious and afraid. I lived a tolerable existence but was exhausted. I was not living the positive and fruitful life that I now recognize we have been created for.

It took me quite a long time to identify myself as insecure and longer still to climb out of what must have begun somewhere in early childhood. While the journey to healing hasn't always been easy, it has been interesting, enriching and freeing!

If people are intended to be emotionally whole, how did I end up so insecure? What pieces to the puzzle of my life could explain my emotional state at age thirty?

A Brief Autobiography

I believe that I was abused as an infant. Whether this has much bearing on my state of insecurity as a child, I do not know. But I have a vague memory of being sexually groped by an elderly relative before age two.

When I was four, my mother returned to work after being a stay-at-home mom. The timing was wrong for me, but it was an exceptional opportunity for her, so I experienced loss and found myself cared for by a short succession of rather unkind caregivers until at age six I went to school full-time. Then a really wonderful woman minded me before school and at lunchtime until I was twelve. I had a relationship with her that was consistent, positive and long-term.

School was bearable and perhaps interesting at first. I was left-handed and forced by my grade one teacher to switch. I then wrestled with reading but conquered the challenge. At age seven I was transferred (to an experimental school that in time would prove a failure) due to changing boundaries. I was content until age nine. Then I experienced ongoing bullying to such a degree that by age eleven I cried daily at school and had no friends in my class. Social survival came with a younger girl next door and friends from another neighbourhood.

Through the bullying I learned compassion but also that telling the truth was not a sufficient weapon against lies and that authorities could turn a blind eye if getting involved was inconvenient. My mother offered to intervene, but, fiercely independent, I believed I had to cope on my own. The bullying only stopped when we all went to junior high and the group of girls from the experimental school were divided into four different classrooms. I was spared any of the old classmates and met and made new friends.

I was raised going to church and had a friend or two in that arena. My clearest memory is of being third choice for the lead in a Christmas pageant and jumping at the opportunity. Evidently the Sunday school leader was surprised that I did a superb job; children will flourish if given opportunities compatible with their talents (I now hold an honours BA in dramatic arts). Without pride and accustomed to ridicule rather than encouragement, I blossomed in spite of the lack of affirmation, although I still fight back tears when I work with children. They are vulnerable and needy and wonderful! How I wish for every child to receive much affirmation!

One deep joy I experience now is to share God with children in ways that I did not receive. Had I been encouraged to have a relationship with God as a child, perhaps I would have been spared much grief. When I finally learned that putting God at the centre of our lives brings heart-healing love, I received the affirmation I needed.

High school offered me a freedom I'd never before experienced. The large number of pupils gave me some anonymity. In class I found myself impervious to criticism of peers and full of joy. I asked too many questions, each of which was sincere; I earnestly sought answers. Teachers usually appreciated the interest, though high achieving pupils in the class were impatient and wanted time at the end of the class to get their homework done.

On the social front, I was naive and wanted intimacy with boys for the affection they could offer so was easy to kiss. I was hurt by female gossip that suggested I did something further.

A 400-mile move after my first year in high school was genuinely traumatic as music and drama courses I desperately wanted were not offered in my new rural school. But my parents were not open to negotiation. We moved, and I was forced into educational surroundings that were less than satisfactory (again).

Throughout my teen years I became aware of a lack of relationship with my father, who, typical of the generation of the time, was remote and emotionally unavailable. I was afraid of him and firmly believed that he disapproved of me. I admired and respected him tremendously, as I did my sister, who was four years my senior. In the nuclear family the person with whom I had the most verbal contact was my mother. Unfortunately, by the time I was a teenager, most of our conversations revolved around tutoring sessions (she was an able English teacher, and I was a poor writer) and arguments over nothing and everything. Ferocious arguments always ended in tears and were never resolved. And in group, when there were barbs aimed at me that I found unkind, I would get upset. Her consistent response was, "We were only teasing."

So, throughout my life until her death, it was my grandmother who was my touchstone. She was uncritical and affectionate and fun-loving. As a child I spent summers with her, and as a teen the family moved to live near her. Although not permissive, I felt she did see beyond my temper and loved me. She, and a cat named Boots, were my real sources of unconditional acceptance. We all need love, and in them some of my needs were met.

I mentioned temper in passing, but truly it deserves highlighting. I was so ferociously temperamental as a teenager that my parents could never perceive me in any other light, even though I did mature past it.

By the time I reached the age of eighteen and was dating a boy whom I would later marry (and divorce), I was confused about love, sex, joy and pain and had no idea who I was or how to relate to others in a healthy way. I was so busy trying to survive emotionally that I had no eyes to see others, no spiritual awareness other than a simple faith in Jesus and a distrust of God.

I give all of these pieces in my life in the hope of triggering connections with you, the reader, to help you to identify how events or experiences in your life might have brought you to a point of recognizing your own insecurity.

Fast-forward through my twenties, when my career was good, although personal relationships with men in particular were desperate. I was still confused and needy. By age twenty-nine I was divorced, single and determined to find some measure of happiness. The saving grace was that I had been born again at age twenty-four. It had a profound immediate effect on my life, the fruit of which would come slowly but surely.

In the years between eighteen and twenty-nine I had studied and become a teacher and was well respected in that role. But my personal life remained unsettled. I had married at twenty-one, full of will and determination that a relationship fraught with problems would work out, and within eighteen months had divorced. Then, contrary to my principles and upbringing, I lived with another man to ensure that the relationship would work, but it did not.

At twenty-four I was brought to my knees, where the Lord, ever patient and kind, met me. I became a committed believer in Jesus Christ. Paul writes in Philippians 2:12 to *"work out your own salvation with fear and trembling."* The summer I turned twenty-four was a new beginning that would lead me back to church, to spending every day reading and praying. I was not shy about my faith and found a Christian psychologist who helped me to understand myself. Indeed, I made an effort to mature spiritually, though at the time I was ignorant of the Philippians 2:12 Bible reference. Because I had turned to the Lord in isolation, I did not recognize a mentor or a tutor who could lead me, theologically or spiritually, through the deep process of sanctification; therefore my progress was slow.

For any who know the Lord but are trying to make it on their own, I encourage you to find a group of trustworthy believers and allow the parts of your life that are ungodly to be revealed. As the light shines on the dark aspects of our lives, we can and will overcome them with the help of the Holy Spirit.

Because I was ashamed of my weaknesses and didn't know how to repent and move on, I didn't grow as a child of God very much during my first years as a believer. I was steadfastly consistent with personal prayer and Bible study. However, healing and freedom are found through relationship and I did not know to deepen my relationship with God or other believers in those early years.

My grandmother died when I was twenty-nine, and so I lost my touchstone. I decided to change my life circumstances at that time, and the first step was to leave teaching and move to New York to study acting. That decision would put me in a more vulnerable position socially, which caused me to discover the very personal need for God the Father and for the Comforter—the Holy Spirit. I had learned to trust Jesus and to ask Him to walk with me. But at that point, I had still to learn to surrender to God's authority and to discover how the Holy Spirit would enable me to do that. Leaving behind all that was familiar to me was the first step in my enablement.

Now, I don't advise anyone to leave home in order to leave behind pain. That is not what I was doing. Rather, I was prayerfully and courageously seeking the personal fulfilment and passion for acting I had always hoped for but had never found.

While in New York I decided not to entangle myself in romantic relationships that could compromise my values. I had learned that a relationship with a man was not what I needed to feel whole, but I was still plagued with the same fear I'd had as a bullied child—that I would not be accepted, would not fit in with my peers.

I believe my fear actually facilitated the situation I most wanted to avoid. When I focused my attention on my lack of confidence with peers, I was hypersensitive and dwelt on any indication of rejection. Acting school was wonderful in the study of the craft, and the journey for me that first year was also a personal investigation into inner truth. But I was plagued by teasing, as I drew myself toward immature and unaccepting people and reacted to their rejection, therefore encouraging it. Fortunately, a core of friends who were believers in Jesus filled the social and emotional needs I had that year in New York.

The following year I went to London, England, for further study, but more out of a sense of destiny than any well-planned decision. Here I hated acting school but found the love of my life (only after surrendering all hope I ever would), who is now my husband and the father of my son. I believe it was no coincidence that, as I followed my instincts by going on that journey to London, I met and was challenged by this God-loving man to deepen my relationship with and broaden my obedience to the Lord.

Only by accepting that challenge did I begin to mature as a Christian, and only then did my journey from insecurity to peace really begin. I made the decision to be baptized by immersion and studied voraciously the Word of God, two choices that sent my learning curve to at least a 45 degree angle and engaged me with the Holy Spirit in a deeply wonderful way. I was content in many ways, yet I was still to discover that I had a mountain of emotional insecurity to climb and conquer.

Fast-forward another ten years. My husband and I began to attend a new church that would be the catalyst to my necessary revelation of the sovereignty of God and the start to overcoming insecurity. The desire of this church was to follow the leadings of the Holy Spirit. Like in all churches, the people were well-intentioned but imperfect. I was still unhealed from the rejection of my youth, and God was to use this place to expose me to such a degree of oppression that I would either learn to overcome or be forever trapped. The sense of oppression was very powerful in this church, but the Word of God is "*sharper than any two-edged sword, piercing even to the division of soul and spirit.*"[3] So too did the spirit of oppression need to be cut out of the atmosphere in this church and out of me.

---

[3] Hebrews 4:12.

I realize that many people have been wounded by the church. But church leaders have a tough job as they seek to pastor congregations. I hold no one responsible for the very real pain I experienced. Rather, God allowed it to bring me to wholeness.

The Beginning: Seeing the Symptoms from a Place of Strength

My husband and I had moved several miles to a new home, and so we had moved to a new church as well. Loaded with insecurity, hope and trust in the divine calling of church leadership, I was in the "honeymoon stage" of belonging to a new church. We had been there for a few months. The teaching was sound, the people were friendly, and the leadership was aiming to bring together and grow a congregation of different nationalities and economic backgrounds. It was (and still is) a great place.

But for me, the honeymoon ended abruptly—like a car smashing into a brick wall—when during a healing meeting one leader invited people to speak. I had a song burning inside of me and believed (and still do!) that music is one form of ministry to bring healing (see 1 Samuel 16:14–23). So with a lot of nervousness but also desiring to offer hope to the suffering I went to the front and sang a spontaneous song from my heart.

I was wary of the responsibility and was cautious to say only words that were comforting and theologically sound. There was no accompaniment, but as a professional singer that was not an issue for me. At the end of the song I handed back the microphone to the leader. There was no applause, nor should there have been. We don't make an offering to the Lord and expect applause. But I did need some eye contact, some kind of encouragement, something to say I had taken a risk and that it was okay to do that. Instead, I was ignored by the leader. He made no eye contact with me, and I heard a deafening silence, the intensity of which gave me a headache. Someone from the congregation came to me privately and thanked me for the song, saying it uplifted her (she was a sufferer of depression), and I was grateful for her kind and reassuring words. But from the leader I received no acknowledgement or feedback. The silence from that leader was never broken, and he moved on to another church a few months later.

This was only the start of a "shunning" in that church, which stifled my enthusiasm. From then on, from many in that church leadership, I sensed that I was tolerated but not embraced as a person. I used my singing ability as part of the worship team, but years later it was suggested that I could not be trusted with a microphone (in case I might say the wrong thing) and that I was often an embarrassment to the leadership.

This sentiment was not universal. Others in leadership encouraged me to persevere and apologized for the rejection I was experiencing. That helped me cope, but the rejection continued to be burdensome and the disillusionment painful.

Although as I write this the wounds have healed, the effect was long-lasting and profound. I felt robbed of my calling and of my joy. I felt denied the opportunity to help others. Most of all I experienced a prejudice I never imagined. Yet I know none of it was meant to hurt me deliberately, and God allowed me the experience to teach me and gave me the ability, wisdom and determination to overcome. Later in the book I shall expand on further revelation I received through living this chapter of my life.

Years have passed, I have since had a child, and our family has moved away from that community. If there was anything for me to forgive, it has been forgiven. I have healed and am grateful for every part of the process God allowed. But the degree of pain I suffered from the oppression that false judgment and unspoken criticism brought, and the lessons I gleaned from it, were important landmarks in my growth to security. Out of that pain and that intense level of oppression, I finally got fed up enough to surrender whole-heartedly to God and give Him my complete respect and obedience, so that He could begin to change me from an anxious, fear-driven person to a secure, love-focused woman of God.

Unconsciously, I had refrained from fully trusting God up to this point because of wrong thinking on two levels. One belief was that I had to protect myself from any outside source, including God. The other was that I could exclude God from my decision-making process. By allowing me the pain of rejection and disillusionment, God broke me of that thinking, and I was truly released into higher, broader and deeper thinking that led to my freedom in Him.

To any who may suffer pain from others' judgments, know that God only allows what you can endure, and He provides the way to overcome. We always have a choice to accept it with grace and learn to overcome it. God will enable you. He actually allows all things in order to teach us and to bring us to a place of surrender so deep that we recognize that only His power and love can save us. The alternative is to allow bitterness or disillusionment toward others to oppress or overpower us.

One other blessing that came from that particular experience with church leadership was the awareness that coming under shame and oppression had been a pattern in my life, that cyclically I experienced rejection that wounded me deeply, causing me to hibernate to lick my wounds. By experiencing and facing the rejection at last, with God's help I was able to overcome it once and for all.

I have returned to my home country of Canada now, and all has come full circle. I first drafted this book in 2004, and it has been a journey of rewrites and new experiences to offer before it was ready for you. Now I believe we are ready to take a journey together, and I wish you every blessing as you dive into the work at hand. God bless you!

One thought I'd like to address before we press on: what status or credentials do I have to suggest that what I have to offer will bring healing? I am a layperson, so it would seem I have little authority to write this book. However, because I've lived with and conquered anxiety and insecurity, I believe what I've learned is useful to those who want to achieve personal freedom and peace of mind.

Paul of the New Testament was a learned man. But his personal claim to authority for teaching the world of his time was not his letters but his suffering.[4] So, while I cannot compare my message or authority with that of a man whose teaching educated and helped to set free a world forever by preaching the gospel of Jesus Christ, I offer my discoveries and victory to others to the degree that I suffered and have overcome.

What matters in our journey to overcoming insecurity is not at all the impression others have of us but rather the impression God has of us. He gives us our identity and will enable us to deal with our shortcomings when they arise. As we analyze our self-worth we can discover what makes us unique. We can learn to appreciate ourselves.

So this is my mission: to share the experience God gave me to inspire others to make their own journey out of the darkness of their insecurity and into the light and freedom of self-acceptance.

It is possible to live in an emotional state of assurance and peace, resting confidently in the knowledge that we are lovable! In fact, not only is it possible; it is meant to be normal for every one of us!

On a practical note, I believe it is best to follow the sequence of Scriptures and summaries presented at the end of each chapter. As you meditate on the Scriptures and apply them to your story, I

---

[4] *Yet indeed I also count all things loss for the excellence of the knowledge of Christ Jesus my Lord, for whom I have suffered the loss of all things, and count them as rubbish, that I may gain Christ* (Philippians 3:8).

trust you will be encouraged and uplifted. We facilitate the journey by taking responsibility for a current situation and avoiding the pitfall of blaming others or making excuses. Only after we have accepted responsibility for our attitude and future can we look at overcoming barriers that may have been created by others.

Finally, a friend who is a medical doctor has reminded me that many emotional aches can find their roots in a physiological medical problem. So it is important to add that there is no substitute for a relationship with your doctor. If in reading this book you find the complete solution, that is wonderful. However, you may also need the advice of a doctor, whose medical or scientific perspective can offer what this book cannot. It would be irresponsible of me to suggest that medicine is not at times a key to healing emotional trauma. In my case it was not overly relevant. However, there were times when words from a counsellor or medical practitioner were invaluable in assuring me that my pain was real and could be overcome.

Each of us will journey uniquely. What this book offers is a focal point to make us aware of our anxiety and a practical strategy to overcome the personal insecurity that binds us.

All direct scriptural quotes are taken from the New King James Version of the Bible unless otherwise stated and are there for meditation and consideration, that we may be built up, with minds renewed by the power of the Word of God. Use them, refer to them and reflect upon them. Jesus said, "*It is the Spirit who gives life; the flesh profits nothing. The words that I speak to you are spirit, and they are life.*"[5]

---

[5] John 6:63.

Section II

Searching for a Remedy
Seeking Security that Lasts

*Therefore, if anyone **is** in Christ, **he is** a new creation; old
things have passed away; behold, all things have become new.*
2 Corinthians 5:17

God wants us to be free from fear, oppression, anxiety and
insecurity—to be who He created us to be. If you can run with me
from this starting block, we've got an exciting race ahead. Each of
us will run at his own pace and win the prize of freedom.

Oppression is the design of the enemy of God, to crush the
life, power and authority of the Holy Spirit, who enables us to walk
in joy, love and peace. We can make the choice to live in freedom.
Once we make that choice, our work begins.

Here's a nugget to start with: whatever you have experienced in
the past is past; the effects of it can be overcome. No one can
change your life for you, but if you want to, you can change your
life for yourself, so that you can be the person you were created to
be *and can enjoy being that person.*

Friends, what a breath of life to be secure, to know you are
loved unconditionally, with freedom to be who you were born to
be! This is the promise of a secure life. This is our hope and our
aim!

The First Step Toward Change Is Awareness

Though we may deny it or be unaware of it, most of us wrestle with a degree of insecurity, of feeling that we must conceal a part of ourselves from the world and live behind a mask—a false self—in order to be acceptable to others. This belief is so ingrained that we accept it is a natural part of our humanity. But it is not!

I wasn't conscious of my insecurity until I began the healing process that would lead me out of it. My insecurity was rooted in the fear that I would be rejected. It robbed me of the sense of inner peace that is meant to be our natural state of mind.

There are two stages to overcoming insecurity. First, we need to recognize our fear—that we don't actually believe we are acceptable as we are, and we are afraid to be "found out." Then we must go on to receive and inhabit the truth that we *are* acceptable. That will lead us to live in the power and authority we were born with. Then we will have that peace that so many in the world chase after through new age and Far Eastern meditations or mood-altering drugs.

Chapter 1

What We Need to Feel Secure

An adult who is secure lives free from fear, accepts who he is, and breathes and moves as he was created to do and be. To be secure is to have inner peace, living in assurance that we are loved *for who we are.* When we are secure, we feel safe, knowing that a bond of trust, mutual affection and acceptance exists between us and those close to us. Security springs out of love, love that is unconditional, unwavering and unending. Therefore the totally secure person knows he is totally loved. Security is dependent then on one thing: the receipt of love.

Suppose our capacity for love could be held in a transparent test tube inside of us. Picture a large empty test tube, the type used in high school science experiments. Imagine it filled to the rim with a liquid, and we'll call the liquid *love.* Now imagine that some of the liquid has evaporated, and the test tube is only partially filled. I believe most of us live as though we have partially filled test tubes and do not realize that it is possible to be filled to the top with affirming, unconditional love. A totally full test tube indicates that we have perfect love, perfect security.* We are fully tanked.

---

*A dry, empty test tube would indicate living in the absence of love.

Security develops through our relationships. The more confident we are in our significant relationships, the more secure—and the more loved—we feel. At that point in our lives the test tube is quite full. If we lack confidence in our significant relationships and don't feel very secure or loved, at those times it's as though our love test tube is nearly empty. Or think of the space instead as a gas tank. As the analogy goes, a car doesn't run far on empty!

How Security Is Developed and Nurtured

When we are born we are hungry for love, even before we are hungry for food, even in the womb. Studies have shown that babies can learn to feel accepted when affectionate words, music and attention are conveyed to them by the parents.

Parental love is our first source of love. We absorb the reaction from Mommy and Daddy, and it shapes our self-image. When we are affirmed during infancy it begins to shape our sense of identity as worthy and acceptable. Then we meet siblings and other relatives, before we develop bonds through peer friendships. Out of each fragile connection we develop an image of ourselves; the significant others around us are "as gods" to us, all-knowing and all-able relative to our level of dependence upon them. As we are affirmed and directed we learn a healthy sense of self and responsibility.

The ideal upbringing is the one where our natural personality is encouraged to develop, and gently but firmly we are given guidelines for social responsibility. But raising a child this way is an art. It is the ideal but is very difficult to achieve, because both child and parent are imperfect, and even the most well-intending parent can misjudge what is innate in a child and what needs correcting.

The Role of My Family

From the beginning, our family is the most influential source to fill our test tube—or our love tank—and therefore to build a healthy identity and sense of security. A family has the opportunity to fill the infant's need for love, the child's need for assurance and the adolescent's need for trust and respect.

When I was growing up, I had an older sister, a mother and a father. I admired my sister, but her message to me was that I was a pest. My mother was good to me but returned to work a year before I started school and so was suddenly no longer always available. My father was a man of integrity but completely absent to me emotionally. These ingredients, and many experiences both within and external to the family, gave me a limited experience of affection, acceptance and love. My love tank never ran above a quarter full! I do not say that my family did not love me; rather I am articulating my experience and my perception.

To compensate for the unsatisfactory relationship with my parents, I had a grandmother who was my best friend, and I connected and felt safe, accepted and loved by her. I had a cat who allowed me to pamper him and was my release for affection. These two sources provided opportunities to learn to receive and to give love in a way I could naturally connect with, and so I was able to develop some sense of security. However, in the absence of a strong sense of love from my immediate family, the substitute feeling of fear filled the remainder of my love tank, and fear (or the absence of love) bred insecurity. In adulthood that fear of judgment would come to influence strongly my actions and self-image.

What Else Can Go Wrong?

There are people who feel unloved even though they have grown up in a tight family unit with loving parents and siblings. Surely security in early relationships guarantees high self-esteem? Family acceptance is valuable to building self-esteem. Yet there is no guarantee that a loving home will produce confident, self-assured offspring or that an orphan won't grow into a confident, emotionally healthy individual. This is because people have different sensitivities to the input they receive from others. There can be a gulf between what is offered and what is received; the best intentioned parents can love a child in a way that does not deeply touch the child.[6] Or an individual can experience rejection outside the family that cannot be counterbalanced at home. This is useful to accept in order to avoid the "blame game," at moments when we might be tempted to blame someone else for not fulfilling our needs. It is healthiest to look ahead, not denying the pain but moving out from under it.

I believe an area of insecurity springs from a negative message received from someone of great significance once, twice or perhaps repeatedly. Children are sponges and pick up every message and filter it through their childlike perceptions. An innocent word from a significant adult can produce a profoundly positive or negative self-image in a child. For example, my son Jordan absolutely adores his "Uncle Jack."[7] If Uncle Jack says anything to him, he takes it as absolute truth. Once when Jordan was three, Jack told him that Englishmen fight against Frenchmen (a condensed history lesson of the Hundred Years' War). The next time he saw Jack and they began to play fight, Jordan said over his laughter, "Stop; I'm English!" (So is Jack, by the way.) No doubt Jack will be completing the history lesson over the next number of years to give a fuller picture to Jordan of the English-French conflict!

Our family friend says only life-affirming messages to our son, but what if he told him he was stupid? Do you think Jordan would defend himself or ignore it? Or would he instead begin to believe the negative message Jack gave him?

---

[6] Gary Chapman Phd, Ross Campbell MD. *The Five Love Languages of Children* (Northfield Publishing, 1997).

[7] *Jack* is a pseudonym, as our friend may prefer to be anonymous.

Whatever message a child receives, be it life-giving or condemning, has a profound effect if the child sees the message-bearer as significant and takes the message seriously. It is far less dependent on the intention of the bearer.

Can you remember words spoken to you when you were young? Trace back to words that were affirming and carried you through difficult times, that built in you a courage that mobilized you to face challenge. Then trace back to words that were crushing, that made you feel inadequate or unable. Words are powerful and leave indelible impressions for a lifetime. Words have the authority to empower or to paralyze. Fortunately we can be healed from critical words and move forward in our journey to confident assurance.

Let's look at Scripture to see how God's Word has power to heal.

How We Are Healed

God's perfect love heals where we have felt rejection, and His Word replaces criticism we've experienced if we allow it.

If parental love were perfect, if family and close friends never rejected us, we could venture from our safe cocoon into a hardened world and make it a warmer place. But human parents aren't perfect. Inevitably, most of us will lack some measure of love almost from the beginning of our lives.

Babies are born into a world needing affirmation, and when the nurture is absolutely perfect, the baby grows in security. But perfection is pretty difficult to achieve. For most of us, in infancy or later in our development, we experienced some measure of rejection. The experience of rejection creates a scar, a "soft spot" that is hypersensitive to future rejection. With further rejection, the scar grows and deepens, developing in us a fear of rejection. Fear is the soil out of which our insecurity grows.

Out of our lack of love we look for more. We will seek and take whatever we can get, so desperate we are for a life-giving source of love.

Where can we find this satisfying, unconditional, predictable and stable source of love? We look for it in other people. But no one is perfectly equipped to give us all we need. By the nature of our humanity, we all have a void and seek its fulfilment for ourselves.

The only source of perfect love is the one perfect person, Jesus.

Scripture tells us we are valuable, a royal priesthood, fearfully and wonderfully made. As you spend time with the following words, speak them out loud, trust they are for you personally, and allow them to replace some of the negative words you have taken in the past. This is a time of healing. Allow these words and God's promise of love to begin to fill that void within you: Psalm 139:14; 1 Peter 2:9; Jeremiah 29:11.

Loving attentive parents, close-knit siblings and an intimate extended family: these provide a strong foundation for building good relationships throughout a lifetime. Close friendships that are authentic, inevitable breakups that are without condemnation or hostility: these are signs of emotional health. When we have peace within and an inner knowing that we are acceptable and lovable, we are grounded, secure.

Summary

We find our source of identity from our immediate caregivers from birth. Their love is the emotional food that ensures our survival.

Unconditional love in sufficient amounts ensures a sense of security. We thrive on it. Like gas to a car, if there is sufficient love, we can run for a long time.

The opinion of anyone who we believe is significant will affect our self-image and sense of security. Our perception rather than their actual impression is what affects us.

The only perfect source of unconditional love comes from God.

Scriptures

> *I will praise You, for I am fearfully and wonderfully made; Marvelous are Your works, And that my soul knows very well* (Psalm 139:14).

> *But you are a chosen generation, a royal priesthood, a holy nation, His own special people, that you may proclaim the praises of Him who called you out of darkness into His marvelous light* (1 Peter 2:9).

> *For I know the thoughts that I think toward you, says the LORD, thoughts of peace and not of evil, to give you a future and a hope* (Jeremiah 29:11).

Chapter 2

Where to Seek What We Need: Human Love and Its Limitations

Let's look at the love available from others to see both its strengths and its limitations, for although human love has limits, it is wonderful to experience and share amongst ourselves. It is our great joy as well as our great need.

What a Healthy Friendship Looks Like

A healthy relationship is founded on mutual trust and respect, and there is an absence of fear. Friends feel free to discuss and share or to be private from time to time. In a healthy friendship each encourages the other person to grow (and is not fearful if the other person changes). Health in friendship shows itself through the acceptance of each other.

Depth of friendship is revealed when each party has the freedom to express deep-felt thoughts, aspirations and secrets and feels safe doing so, confident that even in vulnerability there is mutual respect and caring. Friends can agree to disagree and still be friends, because the relationship is based on love that is deeper than perfect compatibility or agreement. Finally, a friend does not hold a vested interest in what the other chooses but rather allows the other person independence and a separate identity. This kind of relationship we'll call *interdependent*, because there is mutual reliance (but not dependence) between the two people.

This close bond of friendship makes us feel secure, accepted, respected, trusted and loved. We were created to be in relationship with one another. God made man in His image, and then He made woman because it was *"not good that man should be alone."*[8] Relationship gives us a sense of purpose, accomplishment and fulfilment. It is a wonderful expression of who we are when we share moments of our lives with someone else. Accomplishments seem greater and discouragements smaller when we share them with another human being.

But rarely are our significant relationships this transparent. We need to be filled with love, and yet we are ill-equipped to relate. So we strive to sustain our relationships through less-than-total transparency to avoid the pain of isolation and failure. The degree to which we limit our relating is the degree to which there is room for co-dependency, distrust or fear to enter in.

Co-dependency—an Unhealthy Bond

Co-dependency is a type of bonding that occurs when there is insecurity between the individuals.[9] Because one party (or both parties) is insecure in the relationship, he compromises the integrity of his personality in order to protect the friendship. There may be mutual affection and compatibility, and the individuals have fun together. But one (or both) does not feel safe to express who he really is.

Perhaps this is why people more often fight within a family or in marriage, where it is harder to break the bond. There is a

---

[8] *And the LORD God said, "It is not good that man should be alone; I will make him a helper comparable to him"* (Genesis 2:18).

[9] *Co-dependency* is defined as "A set of adaptive behaviours reflecting the individual's absorption with meeting the needs of others to the exclusion of his/her own needs," web definition from Mental Health America, Central Virginia.

measure of perceived security in family that might not exist outside of family, so we more freely expose ourselves to our family, whom we feel perhaps know us best anyway. We are less inclined to hide. Whenever we feel we must hide a part of ourselves to be acceptable, then we sacrifice our freedom, and we forfeit confidence and feel shame instead.

Shame is a powerful oppressor. Where fear makes us anxious and causes us to worry about what awful thing might happen, shame destroys our self-esteem, isolates us and makes us feel unworthy, inferior or depressed. If ever you feel ashamed of who you are or as though you need to change in order to be accepted, you are probably experiencing co-dependency.

Control

With fear of isolation comes the temptation to control or the willingness to be controlled. But this is unhealthy. Control opposes freedom. Control looks at a friend and says, "We need to be the same" while freedom says, "I value you for whoever you are." Although Jesus wept when the Israelite people would not come to Him, He did not try to manipulate them to do as He wanted. *"O Jerusalem, Jerusalem, the one who kills the prophets and stones those who are sent to her! How often I wanted to gather your children together, as a hen gathers **her** chicks under her wings, but you were not willing!"*[10]

Control does not love. It does not trust. It believes it must rule in order to achieve the love that it needs, but it destroys love by trying to extract it. There is no life in control, because it hates life. Life flows out of spontaneous, natural relationship. With control there is no spontaneous, there is no natural. Control stifles freedom and says satisfaction comes from my rule being followed rather

---

[10] Matthew 23:37.

than from anything external, because nothing external can be trusted. Control says, "If I dictate how this relationship runs I will have the love that I need." It does not see the entities as separate life-breathing individuals with hearts and minds but rather as a means to get what it wants. If you wrestle with control in your relationships, you can learn to understand it and to overcome it.

Fear of Man

We were made for relationship, and so we need it. But to choose co-dependent relationship over independence is a high and unnecessary price to pay to avoid isolation. It is natural to resist aloneness, but to fear being alone can control us, and the desire for relationship can overpower our sense of identity and unique purpose.

Fear is anticipating or expecting negative judgment from others. In a healthy relationship we accept the other person in spite of imperfections, and likewise he or she accepts us. When there is a lack of confidence in the friendship, fear suggests that if we do or say something the other person dislikes or doesn't agree with, the friendship may end. When we curtail our behaviour to prevent a perceived threat to the friendship, we are then being dominated by fear of man.

We *fear* that we will be judged and discovered to be not good enough. Naturally, we wish to avoid critical judgment, and so we adapt our behaviour to a given situation or relationship. I believe it is quite universal to live this way, at least within some of our relationships; it is natural to want to make a good impression, and so we put our "best foot forward." But I call living with a heightened state of *guardedness* concerning our encounters *the fear of man*. If we live in a state of high alert, concerned that we will lose approval, be rejected, let others down, be recognized as a failure, make the wrong decision, lose our personal identity, lose our personal value, be recognized for who we really are rather than how we've allowed others to perceive us, or just plain fail, we are living in fear. The best remedy for this is not to try to please people but rather to enter into transparent relationships built on love, respect and acceptance.

Limitations

This chapter is called "Human Love and Its Limitations." One of our limitations as a species is our propensity to judge, for if we judge we too will be judged.[11] Jesus warned us about this because it is natural to us as human beings to do it. However, this inbuilt habit of assessing the behaviour and actions of another has a damaging effect not only on those we judge but on ourselves as well, as we become fearful of judgment from others. This may drive us to be "people pleasers."

Another human limitation is our self-centredness. We love in order to be loved. Rarely are we able to love without an agenda of some kind. Parental love is perhaps the most sacrificial, but even then we can get annoyed at our children and be quite critical. Sometimes they deserve it; always they require guidance. But although we are predisposed as parents toward unconditional love, sometimes we can allow our children's performance to determine our expression or degree of love for them. Even with our children we can be tempted to love on condition we receive from them obedience, success or affection.

Finally, we are limited by our interests, values, compatibility and stamina, and so we cannot be all things to anyone.

---

11 *"Judge not, that you be not judged. For with what judgment you judge, you will be judged; and with the measure you use, it will be measured back to you"* (Matthew 7:1-2).

Why We Do What We Do

We need love for our emotional well-being. We learn early on that to receive love we need to give love. Why then do we not automatically love as Jesus loved, unconditionally and unreservedly?

I think it is because we are living in a state of insecurity; we just aren't able to love the way Jesus loved without first receiving the Father's love as Jesus did. And we have been brought up to be self-sufficient and independent, so we don't necessarily realize we don't have to achieve loving relationships in our own strength.

Self-Image, Self-Contempt

Throughout our lives there will be times when we metaphorically look in the mirror and like who is looking back. Yet at other times, we will decide we need to change something in ourselves that we do not like. When we make those discoveries and decide to change based on our values, then we are taking responsibility for ourselves in a healthy way, and our self-image remains intact. But if we change in order to get approval from someone else, then we are living out of a poor self-image.

Where does our self-image originate? It comes from the messages we have received thus far from others significant to us.

Emotional security is cultivated where there has been sufficient love given, and what grows from it is an understanding that we are "good," "lovable" and "acceptable." Conversely, insecurity grows from the sense that we are not *fully* good, loveable or acceptable, not good enough to warrant the full complement of love and acceptance we need. Then we learn to believe that inherently we lack something required to be loveable. As our need for love is fundamental to our survival, so we are provoked to solve our problem: we aim to be a better person, hoping to earn more love.

Insecurity says that something external to us will make us good, acceptable, whole. For emotional survival we learn to cling to whatever nuggets are offered. These might be relationships that are co-dependent as we bond with other insecure people who cannot offer the nurturing we crave because they are in need themselves. Or we aim high, clinging to those we consider to be of higher status, to try to raise our own profile and our opinion of ourselves. Such friendships are rarely fulfilling.

Choosing unhealthy relationships will diminish our confidence and self-esteem. We need instead to learn to build relationships that will strengthen our self-image and encourage us to love. Those relationships come from others who love and accept and enjoy us simply as we are. Ultimately, no one human being can fulfil our security needs, but as we reach out and offer to others, we will begin to receive encouragement and love.

Human beings are social entities. Relationships are the best means to instil in us a sense of acceptance. However some of us take a different strategy and avoid relationships, instead looking to increase our sense of self-worth through academic, financial or societal success. For example, we may choose to work long hours at our offices and ignore our families to raise our level of self-esteem, when really it is our most intimate relationships that build our true sense of worth. How many lost souls are there in the music, film and modelling businesses who believed they'd find their security in fame and notoriety, only to discover that their loneliness only grows when there is no one with whom to share the "glory"?

Our first step to building our self-esteem (and hence cementing a positive self-image) is to build healthy relationships that offer mutuality of respect, appreciation and love.

Messages Received

Throughout our lives we need relationship. Those that build our self-esteem will be healthier, more transparent and more genuine. The more critical, more judgmental, more distant relationships will not build and may even damage the self-esteem we have. The quality of the relationship determines the message we receive from the other person.

Can you think about your significant relationships? Do they build you up or crush you? Perhaps they are neutral, because you have not experienced emotional intimacy. If we return to the test tube analogy, when looking through the side of your test tube, is there a gap between the top of the liquid and the top of the test tube? If you feel less than perfectly loved or perfectly confident, there will be a gap or hole, a void that naturally seeks to be filled. What will you use to fill it? If love is not there to fill it, it will be filled with the fear of not being loved, because the need for love is so strong that we strive for it, and if it is not available we mourn it. Sometimes we try to cram in all sorts of things to fill this void. But for now, let's focus on our innate response to the void, what I will call "the fear gap"—the fear of not being loved, or the gap between the love we do experience and perfect love.

Insecurity Later in Life

How did we progress from being freely loving and accepting as children to existing as fearful and guarded adults? If like me you had a less than perfect self-image going into adulthood, how you learned to relate was affected by this low self-image. Even if we had a comfortable cocoon and were safe, loved, nurtured and accepted as infants and children, we will still have encountered the big wide world— which can be cruel and critical. And yet much has to do with our family life and how affirmed we were at the baseline. The less affirmed we were growing up, the more vulnerable we'll be to adult rejection, and perhaps the less equipped we will be to deal with it. When we have experienced rejection once (and let's face it: who hasn't!), we realize it could happen again. This potential threat can make us afraid of being hurt again, so we feel apprehensive.

If we deem a new relationship of paramount importance to our emotional survival, *doubt and fear will be stirred in us.* As human beings, we necessarily seek relationship to gain value, and we recognize instinctively that affirmation, when denied us, can make us lose our sense of value. Fear surfaces because we do not want to lose that value. So we can either run from the relationship or distort ourselves to avoid rejection.

No one likes to lose their life's savings. When we invest in our relationships, they are our investment into our self-esteem "bank." We need relationships, and we want to avoid rejection. So we consider, consciously or subconsciously, how we can ensure we will be acceptable. If we decide to modify our behaviour or style of interaction to protect ourselves from rejection, we effectively reject ourselves, in order to protect our image with others.

False Self

At any age, if we attach significance to someone else's opinion of us, we make ourselves vulnerable to rejection. Fear creeps in silently, invisibly, like carbon dioxide filling a car in an air-tight garage. If I elevate someone above me and seek to impress them, I dance with oppression and fear. I have no control over their opinion of me, although I probably act as though I do. I may devalue myself, manipulate my own behaviour and live inside a false self. If my motive is to avoid isolation, I may compromise my integrity or identity to achieve relationship. To avoid rejection, I turn it inward.

I am not talking about changing myself because I see flaws in myself and I need to develop my character—that is growing in maturity. Rather, this kind of transformation is superficial and only has to do with my own need to be loved and accepted. If I hide behind a facade in order to be accepted, I am actually blocking real relationship and genuine acceptance. It is not possible for the false self to receive affirmation; it is only a pretense, and so any acceptance is hollow. And the message to myself if I act disingenuously is "I am not worthy just as I am."

Think of some of the romantic comedies, where the rejected lover adopts a ridiculous exaggerated persona in an attempt to salvage dignity or to attract his target, in a bid to regain affection and self-respect. The sad thing is, in reality people really *do* such things (otherwise we wouldn't laugh at the movie!).

A typical adolescent pursues popularity through his or her style of clothes or choice of music. His motive is to fit in. But he is sacrificing his identity (and security) by making choices or by behaving in ways that don't actually represent who he is. In order to be acceptable to the crowd, he rejects his individuality in exchange for the company of others. Ironically, the company probably consists of others doing the same thing. Living with a false self may prevent physical isolation, but it causes psychological isolation and insecurity.

I used to wear a false self. I would be apologetic when there was disharmony even if I didn't believe I was at fault. If I detected a shadow crossing a friend's face, a panicky feeling would stir inside me. I was anxious and afraid I'd lose a friend, so I would become overtly talkative, smiley, chatty, even flirtatious in order to distract the other from their (possible) hostility—trying to charm him or her to win favour. This was stressful, but just as I believed someone's negative look was caused by me, so also I hoped I could control and dissuade that person from their negativity. Then, as no conflict arose, I believed I had averted conflict, and so my habit to manipulate was reinforced.

If I perceived a cold shoulder from someone, I withdrew into myself, dejected, miserable, tainted by the blow of rejection. This was contrary to my naturally direct and forthright personality. Although no harsh words would be spoken, I would for weeks feel completely isolated and dejected because of one look that was never explained or even confirmed as being aimed at me. In hindsight, to this day I've no evidence that those harsh looks were ever toward me. I suspect my perception came from the experience of being bullied in elementary school, where I developed a self-centred victimization perspective of relationship.

Through all of these behaviours, I was giving away power[12] that should have stayed with me. I was trying to transform my personality but also became intensely fearful that I would be "found out" as phoney. Worry would crescendo into anxiety, and my behaviour became rooted in a reaction to my fears, rather than a natural response to interactions with human beings. For years I was uncomfortable in relating with others and lacked peace and freedom in my relationships.

Building from Life Experience

"Once bitten, twice shy" expresses a natural reaction to rejection. Who of us enters into a second or subsequent romance with the same emotional freedom as our very first? It might be called "puppy love," yet that love is free and full of joy. Young children lack pride and self-consciousness too, perhaps in part because they've not yet suffered as much hurt as an adult has.

Self-Image and Friendship

Human relationships are necessary, affirming and desirable. A healthy self-image will let us build transparent and loving relationships; a poor self-image makes us see others as threatening, with the

---

12 Power, i.e., the confidence within myself to decide whether or not I choose to be connected to a factor external to myself.

power to hurt or to heal us. When we are wounded we live with the message that our imperfection is shameful rather than typical. We live with the fear of abandonment or rejection and struggle with a sense that we are not worthy of love. Even the best human relationships are inferior to a higher source of love, which overcomes all fear.

Summary

A healthy friendship is based on mutual trust and respect and encourages the other person to grow. The best relationships are transparent and free from fear.

Fear of man can make us alter our personality or behaviour to avoid rejection. Controlling another person's perception rather than acting naturally blocks genuine relationship and mutual love.

We all need to coexist, and we all need friendship and love.

Wearing a false self gives us the message that we are not lovable. It hides us from others and does not allow love to develop.

Human love has its limitations, which can be overcome as we develop our relationship with God.

Scriptures

Beloved, let us love one another, for love is of God; and everyone who loves is born of God and knows God. He who does not love does not know God, for God is love (1 John 4:7–8).

"I love those who love me, And those who seek me diligently will find me" (Proverbs 8:17).

*And you will seek Me and find **Me**, when you search for Me with all your heart* (Jeremiah 29:13).

Chapter 3

Changing from People-Centred to God-Centred Thinking: God is the Source of Healing

We need love to be emotionally whole. Ideally, the love we experience will be limitless, unconditional and permanent. But there is only one sure source for this kind of love, and if we take our limited concept of God out of a box we find His perfect gift inside. With God all is possible, including overcoming fear.[13]

The Bible says in 1 John 4:18, *"There is no fear in love; but perfect love casts out fear."* That means when we are safe in our cocoon of love, there will be no room for fear. To make this cocoon we need lots of *the right kind of love*—love that is unconditional and dependable and totally accepting of who we are. To be born again includes being placed back into a womb of God's love and birthed into a new life. Though many of us have been reborn of God, have we recognized that our new life includes healing from all previous emotional scarring?[14]

If we have learned to fear, we need healing. If we've learned to place our reliance and trust in the attitude or opinion of others

---

[13] *"With men **it is** impossible, but not with God; for with God all things are possible."* Mark 10:27

[14] *And do not be conformed to this world, but be transformed by the renewing of your mind, that you may prove what is that good and acceptable and perfect will of God* (Romans 12:2).

towards us and to worry that their opinion will come short of what we hope, then the fear of man is controlling us. Not only that, but since people are, by their very nature, changeable, if ever we have placed our identity in the opinions of other men or women, our source of security has been on shaky, unstable ground. While people are certainly worthy of trust, even with the very best intentions people are fallible and inconsistent. We change our minds all the time! If we put our security within the confines of human relationships, then our emotional security cannot be stable. So we keep plugging away at relationships but need more from them than it is possible to get.

Fear, insecurity and anxiety: all are rooted in a fear of man— a fear of alienating others and a fear of their rejection. Living in fear has put walls around our emotional selves that are meant to protect us, but they actually keep out love and affirmation.

Acceptance from others cannot fill the void, yet self-worth depends on our relationships. Self-esteem does not develop in a vacuum. So what relationship will guarantee us the security we need? A relationship with God is available, and it is completely transparent. He knows us intimately: "*O LORD, You have searched me and known me. You know my sitting down and my rising up; You understand my thought afar off.*"[15] There are no secrets from God.

Also, He takes us just as we are. "*I will praise You, for I am fearfully and wonderfully made.*"[16] We can trust that He loves us as we are.

Putting God into the Equation

"*And you shall know the truth, and the truth shall make you free.*"[17] We are designed to be in a relationship with God. However,

---

[15] Psalm 139:1-2.

[16] Psalm 139:14.

[17] John 8:32.

humanity broke that relationship millennia before were born. Our DNA has "rebellion from God" woven in, and until each of us has that relationship restored and fostered, that void is within us waiting to be filled by God's love.

"For God so loved the world that He gave His only begotten Son, that whoever believes in Him should not perish but have everlasting life."[18] Life springs from the Holy Spirit, and the spirit of man is intended to be in fellowship with Almighty God. If we are born to relate to the God of the whole universe and that relationship is cut off by the very nature of our (sinful) humanity, then it is no wonder that we feel overwhelmingly vulnerable, incapable and insufficient on our own.

When access to God was cut off, humanity learned to replace the relationship with Him with dependence on significant others in our lives for dependence on Him. From birth, these are our parents. Then our siblings and relatives, teachers, friends and colleagues and our own spouses and children become the entities that hold the keys to our sense of acceptance and our security.

Discovering Acceptability

What happens when we acknowledge God as the judge of our character and our personality? We can discover our acceptability and the absolute source of security through Him because He **is** love.[19] He has also said He is unchanging.[20] To what extent are we able to live in the full knowledge of this truth? What deeper

---

[18] John 3:16.

[19] *"God is love"* (1 John 4:8).

[20] *Thus God, determining to show more abundantly to the heirs of promise the immutability of His counsel, confirmed **it** by an oath, that by two immutable things, in which it is impossible for God to lie, we might have strong consolation, who have fled for refuge to lay hold of the hope set before **us*** (Hebrews 6:17-18).

relationship can we find with Him as we seek healing from our insecurities?

What to Do with Fear

When I focus on God's perception of me, I discover that I am accepted. The reference point to finding emotional security is to learn to place my fear in God rather than in man. Why place fear anywhere? Can I not rise above fear? Not really. We are all vulnerable beings, so to recognize that there is power superior to my own is rational. It is not by denying fear that I overcome it but by recognizing it and placing it where it belongs. Living in relationship to God is the only alternative to living with insecurity, because fear is placed rightly in the hands of the most powerful and most trusting source of love.

Let's begin with God's perception of each of us. If true security lies in a sense of being loved, then does God love me? Does He accept me?

God tells us in His Word that we are fearfully and wonderfully made[21] and that we are to love one another.[22] To put it in my own words I'd say, "He thinks we're fantastic and that He wants us to love each other!" If He asks us to love each other then it stands to reason that we must be lovable. As He created us, so it would seem He knows and thinks well of His creation. Further, the fact that He made us makes Him our spiritual Father. We believe and He revives our spirit. This means He is the perfect object to fill the hole a lack of love has created in our lives. He is "Abba"—our "Daddy." Just as a parent offers the most significant influence in the forming of identity, He is the ideal source.

---

[21] "*I will praise You, for I am fearfully and wonderfully made*" (Psalm 139:14).

[22] "*These things I command you, that you love one another*" (John 15:17).

I'd like to share one instance when God's offer of love and security was evident in my life. One day I was walking in sunshine in my small hometown. I was in my mid-twenties. A few days previously I'd been in a counselling session and considering the demise of a love relationship gone wrong. I was learning to recognize that it was not a good, loving relationship, so I was better off now that it had ended. The process was painful, as anyone who has experienced it would confirm. I was a baby Christian at this time.

In the counselling session I had been encouraged to "let go," to shout out my feelings with abandon, rather than be ashamed or hold them in. Well, while on this walk, on this sunny day, in this small town where anonymity was impossible, I suddenly felt compelled to shout, "I'm free!" I think the "shout" was pretty low-key and self-conscious to begin with, but I continued, volume increasing, until I felt (and probably sounded) "free" (or nuts!). I shouted it three or four times, until I had finally expressed myself without being afraid of what other people might think. Folks, I have a loud voice, so I am sure that people indoors probably heard me! But I broke something that needed to be broken that day. In my letting go there was a powerful consequence: not only was I free from a dead-end relationship, but I was also free in my God indeed. I knew if He could love a loud and stressed-out me, then He did indeed truly love me just the way I was. It isn't a groundbreaking story, but I experienced true freedom by trust and action.

Motive: from Control to Trust

Like many of us, I first tasted rejection quite early in life. By adulthood I'd developed three subconscious protective mechanisms to cope, which evolved because of fear of man. These tendencies were to seek to fix a misunderstanding, to explain myself so I could be understood, and to make several apologies for each (perceived) mistake I made.

Each strategy was birthed in anxiety and a desire to control. Each was an effort to maintain relationship and to retrieve a sense of power I'd lost through my fear of rejection. I was motivated by fear and a need to control outcome, rather than by a healthy sense of responsibility in relationship. I was not considering the feelings or needs of others but was totally absorbed in my need for acceptance. I had an over-active sense of responsibility for the success of my relationships, but I was incapable of taking into account the needs of others. I did not "see" others; I assumed that their needs were identical to mine, and my guilty conscience projected my emotions onto them. One root to my fear, I believe, was born from childhood experience.

At eight, I had a best friend. But for reasons I do not recall, at age nine I decided to stop being her best friend. Her reaction was profound. She began to mock me and to tell lies about me to the other girls in our class, and for several years she succeeded in alienating me from my peers. I felt firsthand the rejection of public opinion and the power that acceptance or rejection can have over personal joy and sorrow. This was an early building block to my insecurity and to constructing a defence system against rejection.

If you have faced similar experiences, then it's possible that you also have constructed a survival strategy based on early insecurity that is now irrelevant and unnecessary. If you can pinpoint what those mechanisms or strategies are, you can begin to break habits of a lifetime that inhibit rather than build relationship now.

For me, further rejection came during teen years. So in adulthood my chief aim was to avoid rejection at any cost. My protective strategy was to mask my true self (which I knew was flawed) and put forth a positive image. To build emotional security, my strategy was to win friendship with all people I encountered[23]

---

[23] *If it is possible, as much as depends on you, live peaceably with all men* (Romans 12:18).

and then to secure their acceptance by taking all responsibility for the relationship. The burden of apology always fell to me, so that I could always define the parameters of contact and could keep people on my side. Although none of this was conscious, it was nevertheless disingenuous, and it trapped me in my fear.[24] I had no feeling of being accepted, because I didn't trust my own personality, let alone the loyalty or affinity of others towards me. Furthermore, I did not allow room for others to give to me. I shouldered the responsibility for contact, so beneath the surface was always the question "Is this person choosing to be with me?" My self-esteem was low.

If I analyze my motive, the logic operating within my subconscious was "If I take all responsibility for interaction with others, I can alter or control conditions in relationships, thus avoiding offence on the one hand and rejection on the other." I persuaded myself that to apologize for every oversight between myself and another person would keep peace and deepen communication between us. But this motive was purely selfish, to protect myself from rejection. Love at this level is self-centred and limited, because it is an immature love based on need. It is a love that can only take. Love grows from giving, and so relationships that exist between those who live with insecurity are relatively shallow. But with the love that gives, great depths of understanding and mutual comfort between two people are achievable. Emotional gulfs can be crossed, and great hope, health and truth will blossom when there is no fear.

Be spurred on, all who seek to overcome insecurity! As you discover your motives, you may at first feel disappointment and humility, but you will have satisfaction and joy as you heal and

---

[24] *Keep your heart with all diligence, For out of it* **spring** *the issues of life* (Proverbs 4:23).

overcome your self-centredness or naive, short-sighted limitations.[25] "*When pride comes, then comes shame; But with the humble is wisdom.*"[26]

Swapping Control for Surrender

A specific outcome of emotional insecurity is the desire to control the attitudes of others toward us. It is impossible, futile and, quite frankly, stupid. As much as we might attempt to manipulate, ultimately it causes frustration because it is unachievable. Yet deep down, many of us know no other way.

Getting God's perspective[27] will lead us away from the temptation to manipulate or control others or our relationships. We need His view of us; there is no need to control the opinions of others. As we familiarize ourselves with the person God says He is in the Bible, we will also begin to discover His opinion of us, and we will be able to receive His acceptance—which is an expression of His love for us. When we find God not only as Saviour but as Father, Lord and intimate friend, we discover for ourselves that we have been made well by the master builder and are a new creation in Him.[28]

In my journey from fear to freedom I met Jesus and became a Christian. Yet it took almost twenty years more to achieve release

---

[25] *My son, do not despise the chastening of the LORD, Nor detest His correction; for whom the LORD loves He corrects, Just as a father the son **in whom** he delights* (Proverbs 3:11-12).

[26] Proverbs 11:2.

[27] *In the beginning was the Word, and the Word was with God, and the Word was God. He was in the beginning with God. All things were made through Him, and without Him nothing was made that was made. In Him was life, and the life was the light of men. And the light shines in the darkness, and the darkness did not comprehend[a] it.* (John 1:1-5).

[28] *Therefore, if anyone is in Christ, **he is** a new creation; old things have passed away; behold, all things have become new* (2 Corinthians 5:17).

from the fear of man. Why did it take so long? It took me a long time to fully trust God, and for a long time His promises of unconditional love fell on deaf ears. It also took work to change my habits and perceptions. It was only when I discovered a healthy fear of God that I began to overcome my fear of man.[29] As I learned to trust Him and to accept His opinion of me, I felt His peace and loving reassurance. For each step forward I made a specific personal decision as a believer and follower of Jesus Christ. I chose to trust, to obey and to believe His words in the Bible, and through that process I also overcame insecurity.

I have had a few radical life-changing moments in my journey of faith. One such moment was my decision to trust God 100 percent. I had been a believer for about ten years. I was in a discipleship training program, growing as I learned more about God's Word and the power of His Holy Spirit. During a weekend retreat with the pastor leader and about six others in the discipleship training program, I encountered God in a bizarre and rich moment, thick with the power and presence of the Holy Spirit. The group had been praying for over an hour together in a small basement room. Suddenly, we all began to react in sincere yet unusual ways, breathing deeply, shouting or crying profoundly. I think some were even laughing, expressing the pure joy of the Holy Spirit.[30] I felt a deep, undeniable awareness of God and His truth.[31] I was deeply convicted that I did not fully trust Him. I recognized that He had, at that time, only about 10 percent of my trust. I felt as though I stood at a

---

[29] *The fear of the LORD is the beginning of wisdom, And the knowledge of the Holy One is understanding. For by me your days will be multiplied, And years of life will be added to you* (Proverbs 9:10-11).

[30] *But the fruit of the Spirit is love, joy, peace, longsuffering, kindness, goodness, faithfulness* (Gal. 5:2).

[31] *Into Your hand I commit my spirit; You have redeemed me, O LORD God of truth* (Psalm 31:5).

precipice in my relationship with God and He was asking me to trust Him 100 percent. It was the first time He challenged my relationship with Him as my Father and as my Sovereign. It took every ounce of faith poured out by the Holy Spirit[32] at that moment, but I chose to give Him my trust. It was a conscious decision. Immediately afterward I experienced relief, ease, warmth, comfort and finally a release from the anxiety I'd always lived with. It was the first deeply spiritual moment I can recount in my journey; others would follow. Secure in my trust of Him, I began to accept His love, without wearing my self-imposed conditions of acceptability.

Discovery of His deep and profound love continues.

On to Maturity

Before I grasped and began living the truth that "*the fear of the Lord, that is wisdom,*"[33] I lived with a neurotic fear of people's perception of me. No man has power except what we give him. In my case, I had given all my power away—to friends, strangers, employers, colleagues, professors, teachers and family members. When I chose to believe and follow the Lord, I began a long process to transfer my fear of man's opinion for God's power and authority in my life.

Eventually, I grew to put God's perception above others' including self-perception and listened for Him to point out my strengths and areas needing improvement. But that came only when there was no emotional cost[34] and only when I was keen to

---

[32] *But the fruit of the Spirit is love, joy, peace, longsuffering, kindness, goodness, faithfulness, gentleness, self-control. Against such there is no law* (Galatians 5:22-23).

[33] *"And to man He said, 'Behold, the fear of the Lord, that **is** wisdom, And to depart from evil **is** understanding"* (Job 28:28).

[34] *...God is faithful, who will not allow you to be tempted beyond what you are able, but with the temptation will also make the way of escape, that you may be able to bear **it*** (1 Corinthians 10:13).

grow in the direction He would steer me, toward maturity and grace toward others.

Ultimate success in our ability to *overcome* lies in our answer to the following question: Will we accept God and His love?

Living in Acceptability

Whether our fear is based in reality or the imagination, fear is a state of mind.

If we fear God, that means we respect, elevate, esteem and worship Him. To give God our trust, we allow our security to lie within His power. We must know *who* this God is that we choose to trust if we are to know that it is safe to trust Him with our identity.

God is good, His love is selfless, and He is all-powerful, so we can rest assured that "*the LORD your God is with you wherever you go.*"[35]

God is honourable, and because of this, when He promises to accept us, we are assured that, to our very essence, we are acceptable. We do not have to jump through figurative hoops to please—or appease. God is unchanging and consistent,[36] so His opinion of us won't change depending on our relationship with Him, our behaviour or circumstances. God is consistent, as is His love, acceptance and affection for us.

What a relief! Just as insecurity has eaten away at our confidence, exposing our inadequacies, so does recognizing God's

---

[35] "*Have I not commanded you? Be strong and of good courage; do not be afraid, nor be dismayed, for the LORD your God is with you wherever you go*" (Joshua 1:9).

[36] *Thus God, determining to show more abundantly to the heirs of promise the immutability of His counsel, confirmed it by an oath, that by two immutable things, in which it is impossible for God to lie, we might have strong consolation, who have fled for refuge to lay hold of the hope set before us* (Hebrews 6:17-18).

assurance show us that we are lovable and acceptable. Living in God's affection, holding a reverent fear or awe of Him, and recognizing His sovereignty means we know that there is nothing greater to fear. We are protected, guided and led by Him. He knows our best interests.

Tainted Image of God

Unfortunately, the image some of us hold of God is marred. If we are to find our security in Him as a stabilizing force, we have to change our perception of Him to that of the God of love and justice He describes Himself to be.

How do we do that? How do we come to a place of recognizing God's love for us?

To start, we read it in the Bible, and we accept it in our minds. But for it to live in us, we need *to open our very vulnerable hearts* to trust the acceptance God has for us. Only then will we be able to overcome the fear of man that currently occupies our minds.

Will we choose to trust Him completely? By faith, we have chosen to follow Him, but are there aspects to ourselves we still hide from Him? I certainly did. But through deep searching into His word, time spent alone with Him in prayer, sound teaching and good fellowship—these were the ways He revealed Himself to me in greater depth. I encountered such love! And over time, He gave me the self-awareness and the courage to surrender absolutely everything of myself to Him. It has taken me years just to begin to comprehend Him. But it began with the choices that I made. If you are dubious or frightened of the process of opening yourself completely to God, I can only testify that there is no risk. He will love you, guide you, and strengthen you to be the person He created you to be.

The Sales Pitch

Ultimately each of us must decide how deeply we choose to trust and respect God. The journey will be adventurous and far beyond merely a change in attitude. This journey is a change not only of the mind but also of the heart. It is an adventure that will set you on a course of joyous, challenging and harmonious living.

Change is never easy. It is not for the faint-hearted. Nothing of value ever is. But here is hope beyond your wildest imagination and power greater than any on earth: the power (and love) of God in your life that enables you to be free from fear.

By the power of the Holy Spirit I can declare, you will be changed—because God's Word does not return void.[37]

God's Promises

"The fear of the LORD is the beginning of wisdom."[38] God's word says repeatedly, "do not fear" and yet fear seems to be an integral part of our humanity. I have learned as I trust God and fear only Him, I rise above the circumstances or the thinking that is provoking me to fear. If I don't fear God, it seems I fear something (or someone) else. It's unavoidable.

No man is an island. We were made to be in relationship, and ultimately it is not possible to be completely secure and completely alone. By believing and trusting God, the immutable, unwavering Creator who promises never to leave us or forsake us, we have security.

---

[37] *So shall My word be that goes forth from My mouth; It shall not return to Me void, But it shall accomplish what I please, And it shall prosper **in the thing** for which I sent it* (Isaiah 55:11).

[38] Psalm 111:10a

I've said to fear seems inevitable. Chinese religion is based upon ancestral worship and fear. The Chinese tradition recognizes the power of unseen forces and seeks to appease those forces through worship. When the Chinese hear the gospel of Jesus Christ, they often are quick to embrace it and Him, because they discover His love alongside His power. They embrace Christianity. While ancestral worship is based on fear, true Christianity is based on love. The Chinese tradition has the reality of fear but misses the security of love. When they hear the gospel of love, they embrace it!

Perfect love casts out all fear,[39] and God is love. With the perfect love of Jesus, our fear of God is balanced with His unconditional love for us, demonstrated in His sending Jesus to die for us. We can live secure.

I walked as a believer for years carrying emotional insecurity. Why? Because I did not fear and trust God as much as I feared and wanted man's love and acceptance. My focus was on me. Now I've put my focus on God.

Life is a learning curve. I hope to make the learning curve of others steeper so society can be filled with more secure, emotionally healthy people, walking in the confidence and power that belief and trust in God can give. Then we can be the powerful forces for life and good that we were created to be.

In her book *Women of the Frontlines,* author Michal Ann Goll summarizes,

> Courage arises out of the security of knowing who God is and who we are in relation to Him. We can take courage in the Lord, not because of who we are or what we have, but because of His indwelling presence with us through

---

[39] *There is no fear in love; but perfect love casts out fear, because fear involves torment. But he who fears has not been made perfect in love* (1 John 4:18).

the Holy Spirit. By ourselves we are weak, and can do nothing. But because He dwells in us, we have His power, wisdom and courage…Courage comes out of glorying in our own weaknesses and resting in His strength.[40]

Summary

Emotional insecurity is rooted in a fear of man's thoughts and opinions of us.

By exchanging our unhealthy fear of man for the awareness and fear of a loving God, we are led to emotional security.

A perpetual state of fear-based insecurity is neurotic.

The fear of man is demonstrated in our giving to others the power and authority to judge our behaviour, and it places the concept we have of ourselves at their mercy.

Scriptures

There is no fear in love, but perfect love casts out fear. For fear has to do with punishment, and he who fears is not perfected in love. We love, because he first loved us (1 John 4:18–19, RSV).

Study to shew thyself approved unto God, a workman that needeth not to be ashamed, rightly dividing the word of truth (2 Timothy 2:15, KJV).

---

[40] Michal Ann Goll, *Women on the Frontlines* (Shippensburg, Pennsylvania: Destiny Image Publishers, Inc., 1999), 26.

Section III

Receiving the Remedy
God Is the Source; the Holy Spirit Fills the Void

Chapter 4

The Grace of God

As an act of grace, God offers His love to us freely; it is not based on merit but on the sacrifice of Jesus, God's son.

While insecurity dictates that we must achieve acceptability derived from the good perception others have of us and that acceptance must be earned—the concept of grace smashes this thinking!

When we believe in the sacrifice of Jesus Christ, it is through this faith that we are able to believe that we become children of God. We inherit all of the promises God gave to Abraham and to all His people. We are made "right" with God.[41] God is love. He is abundantly generous. He lavishes love on us who believe with the faith He gave to us, through the sacrifice He made for us. What can better demonstrate God's unconditional love to us than His grace? And nothing of this love comes from who or how we are, but from who and what He is. The person who lives under grace knows he is accepted regardless of his behaviour or interactions. A wise person will not abuse or take for granted that grace;[42] but nevertheless, by its very nature, grace is freely offered, freely given.

---

41 *"Abraham believed God, and it was accounted to him for righteousness"* (Romans 4:3b).

42 *"What shall we say then? Shall we continue in sin that grace may abound? Certainly not! How shall we who died to sin live any longer in it?"* (Romans 6:1-2).

To realize the full consequence of God's grace in our lives, it is helpful to first understand the sovereignty of God. When I began to apply the principle of God's sovereignty over my life and to experience the authority of His truth, my apprehension and my insecurity with people evaporated.

The Sovereignty of God

Sometime in childhood a cloud crossed over my life and remained above me. Sometime in adulthood I became aware of this cloud. That was the beginning of change, because when we know there's a cloud, we also know the sun is somewhere above it. Awareness is the key to moving out from under the cloud and learning to live in the glory of direct sunlight. My discovery of the cloud and understanding of the sovereignty of God did not come about at the same time, but both were necessary in my healing process.

About eight years ago, I was sitting in a church pew, in the front row as it happens, one Sunday morning. A loving and sound pastor was preaching. I don't remember precisely what he was preaching about—it was not about sovereignty—but as I listened a thought came to me: *God is sovereign.* I'd known in my head the truth of this. But it was about to hit my heart and so change my perspective of life that it would be the key, at last, to setting my mind free.

The sovereignty of God implies that He rules the universe and that nothing occurs on earth outside of God's permission or awareness. No event happens without His foreknowledge and His assent to it happening. Everything that takes place occurs in His wisdom and for His ultimate purpose, for His glory and for His goodness. If not, then God would not be God.

What comfort I take from that, and oh, how it hit me that day!

The revelation of this made me realize that the cloud over me had existed for good purpose and that God was in charge of every event of my life to bring me to the realization, not only of Him, but also of His authority over my life. The application of this in my life meant that I did not need to fear rejection but rather could embrace every event, every relationship, as coming directly from the Master Builder, who knew how to build my life into a strong and mighty force for right.

"*We know that all things work together for good to those who love God, to those who are the called according to **His** purpose.*"[43] I realized as I sat in that church pew on that particular Sunday morning that no circumstance could come my way that was not under God's umbrella of protection. I would need to learn how to surrender decisions to His will and His Word, in a consistent and faithful way.

As I deepened my understanding of the significance of God's sovereignty in my life, fear left me. I realized that people did not have authority over my life, but God did. God knew about all the relationships and experiences that would arise in my life, and I could trust the outcome to Him. Another of God's promises is "*For I know the plans I have for you, says the LORD, plans for welfare and not for evil, to give you a future and a hope.*"[44]

Logically speaking, as God is sovereign, then anything that happens happens for God's purpose, and I can learn from it. As God is most interested in His relationship with each of us and the development of our character,[45] He allows circumstances to be presented to us for our good and for our development as followers of Jesus. Recognizing His sovereignty in my life implies

---

[43] Romans 8:28.

[44] Jeremiah 29:11, RSV.

[45] *But also for this very reason, giving all diligence, add to your faith virtue, to virtue knowledge, to knowledge self-control, to self-control perseverance, to perseverance godliness, to godliness brotherly kindness, and to brotherly kindness love. For if these things are yours and abound, **you** will be neither barren nor unfruitful in the knowledge of our Lord Jesus Christ* (2 Peter 1:5-8).

that whatever circumstance might arise, God is (and has been) aware of it; therefore I need not fear or worry about the future or other people's opinions or attitudes toward me interfering with that future. God will always lead me to a positive resolution as I surrender to Him.

Not all circumstances will be easy. That isn't in His promises. But rarely does anything worthwhile come without effort, pain or struggle. *"More than that, we rejoice in our sufferings, knowing that suffering produces endurance, and endurance produces character, and character produces hope."*[46]

Since my revelation and application of God's sovereignty in my life, I have experienced magnificent release. I have faced fear of man and my own fallibility in relationship and have found challenge, growth and peace. Beginning that day while sitting in the church pew, I took a giant leap toward emotional security and have aimed to do the following: *"Forgetting those things which are behind and reaching forward to those things which are ahead, I press toward the goal."*[47]

The revelation that God is sovereign, and that in His sovereignty lies our opportunity for growth, chases away the fear of failure and fear of rejection that embody emotional insecurity. It does not promise that everything will always go our way or that all our relationships will be trouble-free. That is fantasy. But it does ensure that when we know and trust God's authority and power we can choose to rest, confident that all circumstances are for our benefit. Nothing can isolate us or harm us.

A positive attitude based in this truth will yield the sense of security you seek, because you know the Creator of the universe is watching over and guiding your steps. You have given up control,

---

[46] Romans 5:3-4, RSV.

[47] Philippians 3:13b-14a.

that imaginary self-protective strategy, and yielded that illusion of control to the one and only who has ultimate power and authority over the universe that He created.

Tragedy and disappointment are inevitable in life, and events do occur that seem cruel or beyond our understanding. But as He foreknew us, so He also knows what will perfect us. *"But those who wait on the LORD Shall renew **their** strength."*[48] By choosing to trust God and to recognize His ultimate authority in our lives, we are protected by Him and will ultimately triumph over every adversity we face.

The Grace of God

Once I internalized the reality of God's sovereignty over the universe and accepted it in my life, I then began to absorb more of the reality of God's grace.

Grace is receiving goodness we don't deserve. We do not earn it. I knew this theology, but as with sovereignty, knowing these facts in my mind was not equivalent to living with it in my heart. Now I began to recognize for myself the truth that "I do not have to *do* anything (or to *be* anyone) to be saved from anxiety and despair." God gave me the faith to believe in Him, and with that same faith I am saved from oppression, despair and fear, by His grace. He made me; He loves me as a perfect father loves even his wayward son.[49] I could do nothing to earn God's love, nothing to keep it. I have heard Gerald Coates, leader of the Pioneer House Church movement in Britain, convey on a number of occasions, 'There is nothing you can do to make God love you more; there is nothing you have done to make God love you less.'

---

[48] Isaiah 40:31a.

[49] The story of the prodigal son, his father and elder brother, Luke 15:11-32.

Absorbing this personally, I realized finally that the very core of my being was accepted, and my security lay in the revelation and acceptance of that truth.

I'd like to address those believers of evangelical church roots in particular. In your desire to *be* "a good Christian," be sure you haven't inadvertently yoked yourself to the law of *doing* good works (or *being* a "good" person). A condemning message can seep in that while our faith is sufficient for salvation, it is not quite enough just to believe; we must "be" better than we are and "do" more for the church. While practical good works are essential to demonstrating God's love, we can feel driven (by our own consciences or by our well-meaning church leaders) to "do" for God—to evangelize, to witness, and to be "nice" *in our own strength*, out of duty and through a feeling of pressure. But Grace says, be who you are; surrender to the Holy Spirit, and He will teach you and transform you to be more like Christ. Then and only then will you be free to "do" the works of God. So often I have seen myself and others get it the wrong way around: we *do* in order to be righteous and acceptable, rather than *be* in order to learn (from the Holy Spirit) how to do good things.

At the time of my revelation on the church pew, I was in attendance at my evangelical church. I had frequently felt amongst that body a pressure to perform in order to achieve for God. Not only is this categorically unbiblical, it also leads to exhaustion, fear and oppression. Up until that moment of revelation in the pew, I had known I was saved, born again, on my way to heaven, but I did not live as though that were true.

What I began to learn that Sunday morning, during the evangelical church service, is that it is by the Holy Spirit, and only by the Holy Spirit, that we can do these works. If we surrender and seek to be led by the Holy Spirit, He will lead us to do good things; our part is in the surrender. We are not to force ourselves to do good because we "should"—this is living under law and not under grace, with the motive to ensure our acceptance rather than to live in what we have been freely given: "...*if you become circumcised, Christ will profit you nothing. And I testify again to every man who becomes circumcised that he is a debtor to keep the whole law. You have become estranged from Christ, you who* **attempt** *to be justified by law; you have fallen from grace.*"[50]

Living with God under law is just like we live with man, seeking after His approval and acceptance. The reality is that we *already have* His approval and acceptance. He wants us to live in it, to enjoy it, rather than try to earn it. Jesus contrasts God's love with that of a human parent, who may want to do well by his child but is limited; God can do so much more.[51] Surrendered to Him, we will do that which is pleasing to Him, but in His strength and the character He has grown in us, and in His time. We do not need to try to prove ourselves to Him.

God's grace is readily available to free our minds from burdens and heavy yokes, including satisfying others' expectations and our feelings of inadequacy. If we work to please Him, or any man, we will fail. But if we recognize His grace given to us and that He is already pleased with us because He made us, and if we live surrendered in order to learn and to grow in character and understanding and love, we will carry an attitude of fearless confidence. Ironic, isn't it, that we have to be humble enough to recognise our inability to achieve in order to attain the confidence to know we can! Our freedom—the freedom from the insecurity that plagues

---

[50] Galatians 5:2b-4.

[51] "*Or what man is there among you who, if his son asks for bread, will give him a stone? Or if he asks for a fish, will he give him a serpent? If you then, being evil, know how to give good gifts to your children, how much more will your Father who is in heaven give good things to those who ask Him!*" (Matthew 7:9-11).

any person who lives the impossible task of pleasing others in order to find acceptance, peace of mind and freedom from doubt—becomes transparent and a mighty witness of God's gospel of power and love.

By the end of the Sunday morning service, I rose from that pew fully aware that God loved me and that it was He rather than fallible man who had ultimate authority over what would happen to me in this life, and that I did not have to *do* anything from then on to keep my salvation or God's "approval." I have chosen to live in remembrance of what I discovered that day.

I walked out of church, after nearly two decades as a born-again believer, lighter, finally free from condemnation and the insecurity it had propagated in my life.

> *I beseech you therefore, brethren, by the mercies of God, that you present your bodies a living sacrifice, holy, acceptable to God, **which** is your reasonable service. And do not be conformed to this world, but be **transformed by the renewing of your mind**, that you may prove what is that good and acceptable and perfect will of God.*[52]

Summary

Unconditional love smashes insecurity.

Trusting God's sovereignty gives us the assurance all things work toward our good, and there is no need to fear circumstances or people.

Grace is given not earned, and in recognizing this we are free from the burden of perfection in the eyes of others.

---

[52] Romans 12:1-2, emphasis added.

Only by the power of the Holy Spirit can we become Christlike, perfect. We do not, in fact we cannot, do it in our own power; nor is it reasonable to expect us to.

Scriptures

*"Come to Me, all **you** who labor and are heavy laden, and I will give you rest. Take My yoke upon you and learn from Me, for I am gentle and lowly in heart, and you will find rest for your souls. For My yoke is easy and My burden is light"* (Matthew 11:28-30).

"…My grace is sufficient for you, for My strength is made perfect in weakness" (2 Corinthians 12:9b).

Now may the God of hope fill you with all joy and peace in believing, that you may abound in hope by the power of the Holy Spirit (Romans 15:13).

Chapter 5

Mental Roadblocks to Overcoming Insecurity

There are two ways of thinking that are counterproductive to our transformation from fear to confidence: one is putting a high value on financial or career achievement and success; the other is thinking that we must hide our mistakes.

Roadblock I: Achievement

Our attitude to success can leave us vulnerable to insecurity.

Recognizing ourselves as people of value includes having the freedom to fail, to make mistakes, to be vulnerable and mortal. Celebrating success is terrific, but to be oriented to that is a trap. Do we place importance on achievement or success? Will our attitude enhance or strangle the root of our security? To avoid the trap, we need to know that we are more than the net total of our successes.

From Doing to Being—A Shift from Current Culture

We live in a "doing" culture, a culture of "success." What we do well is rewarded, while failure often results in being sidelined. If we gauge our value on external factors such as financial success or fame, we will celebrate achievements but be devastated when failure comes. When our identity is measured by our achievements, our positive self-image is conditional. So, is there a standard we can choose that will redefine our identity and that allows our self-image to stay intact regardless of circumstances or achievement?

Typically, the opening question following an introduction is "What do you do?"

Wouldn't it be great if instead we asked, "Who are you?" or "What's important to you?" Instead we imply "By what means of industry are you valued?"

Our "doing" culture has dictated to us a value that is based on our achievements: our status, our job. Just as our self-esteem is threatened when it depends on someone else's opinion of us, so it is when we attach our image to our accomplishments. Such self-esteem is hollow because it is based on an external value that says nothing about who we are but only what we do.

Can we make a paradigm shift and use *character* instead of *successful achievement* as the unit of measurement? If what we learn or who we become matters the most to us, we will be more in line with God, who encourages us to recognize His standards for character as the highest achievements to reach for. By His grace we are totally acceptable as we are, and yet paradoxically He works to transform us into the person He originally created us to be. During the lifelong process, we rest in the security of His unconditional love, knowing that regardless of success or failure, regardless of how the world views us or even how we view ourselves, God has a good opinion of us. When our attention is on God's perspective rather than on the world's, we are fortified.[53]

---

[53] *Therefore we also, since we are surrounded by so great a cloud of witnesses, let us lay aside every weight, and the sin which so easily ensnares **us**, and let us run with endurance the race that is set before us, looking unto Jesus, the author and finisher of **our** faith, who for the joy that was set before Him endured the cross, despising the shame, and has sat down at the right hand of the throne of God* (Hebrews 12:1-2).

Character

Since we need to value character transformation above all else, what character traits are we to value, and how do we come by them? The benchmarks of godly character are summed up in the following: *"But the fruit of the Spirit is love, joy, peace, long-suffering, kindness, goodness, faithfulness, gentleness, self-control. Against such there is no law."*[54] Because of God's grace and the Holy Spirit within us, when we value these qualities and as we enable them to develop in us, our self-esteem grows. As we are more at peace with ourselves, our lives will become more in harmony with others around us, and our confidence will grow through that as well. Character develops as we surrender to the Holy Spirit rather than working from our own effort, and it is available to those who believe their hearts need an overhaul and seek it. Seeking peace will bring us peace; seeking love will make us more loving. We exchange the trap of the success culture for the "growth culture," where being transformed into who God created us to be is the aim.

Roadblock 2: Hiding Prolongs Shame

While we may think hiding our mistakes buries our weaknesses, it actually creates in us a sense of shame and perpetuates our sense of insecurity. Only the truth will set us free.[55]

Personal Shame: If we hide our deficiencies and failures, we are not living truthfully. If we do not live transparently but instead hide our weaknesses, we are inviting a feeling of shame. While we do not have to advertise our weaknesses and deficiencies (of which we all have many), to bury them, deny them or be embarrassed by

---

[54] Galatians 5:22–23.

[55] *"And you shall know the truth, and the truth shall make you free"* (John 8:32).

them reveals a lack of self-acceptance. If we judge ourselves, we cannot overcome insecurity.[56]

I did not always use personal growth as the measuring rod for my successes. My confidence took a nosedive when I left teaching to study acting. I learned to be ashamed of myself because I did not achieve what I considered success in an acting career.

Although I had a proven track record as a performing arts teacher, I got little work after my own training as an actress and acceptance into the Actor's Equity Association. Whenever anyone would ask me what I did, I hated to reply, because I knew they'd then ask, "Oh, what shows have you done?" or "Have I seen you in film?" While their sincere enthusiasm was intended as encouragement, I felt discouraged. I still shy away from talking about that time in my life and am glad that I have moved on, because what I did was not the sum total of who I was.

The pull to succeed is very strong in our society. For me that meant that there was still a sense of relative failure in those years spent as an actor, irrespective of what skills I developed as a performer, what lessons I learned about others and myself, or who I grew into as a result of that time in my life. When I put that decade into the full picture of the rest of my life, that season was vital to my spiritual journey. I learned a great deal about generosity, peace and self-control, and I learned to accept and to celebrate the experience rather than look for fame or financial gain.

Yes, I've overcome insecurity, but that doesn't mean that, from time to time, I haven't had to remind myself that I am not the equivalent of my accomplishments. Security is not found in a successful outcome but rather in a healthy respect for the process and experiences of life.

---

[56] *"Judge not, that you be not judged"* (Matthew 7:1).

Perfectionism and Pride: A Combination That Blocks Progress

There is an unhealthy tendency that puts an impossible burden on anyone wanting to overcome insecurity. Perfection determines to make no mistakes; pride shrinks from admitting them. But producing one flawless outcome after another is not only a heavy burden but does not satisfy our hearts' need for love and acceptance. And if we expect perfection in ourselves, how will our self-image cope with inevitable failure? Our pride makes it difficult to accept our weaknesses and to learn from them.

Let's look at Peter. From his behaviour we would conclude that Peter was neither a perfectionist nor proud. He made mistakes. He was impulsive, and yet his journey shows that when weaknesses were exposed, it led to healing, transformation and new life.

A Biblical Example of Transformation

After the crucifixion, Peter demonstrated how transparency enables healing. Peter, who walked with Jesus, had the most reason to feel ashamed at the crucifixion, because he denied his friend. He had been a committed friend and follower of Jesus. The Scriptures record him as recognizing the Christ, the Messiah, in Jesus,[57] daring to have faith to walk on the water to Him.[58] Jesus had commended him.[59] Peter had no lack of boldness or enthusiasm. But after the arrest of Jesus, it was the demonstrative Peter who backed

---

[57] *He said to them, "But who do you say that I am?" Simon Peter answered and said, "You are the Christ, the Son of the living God"* (Matthew 16:15-16).

[58] *And Peter answered Him and said, "Lord, if it is You, command me to come to You on the water." So He said, "Come." And when Peter had come down out of the boat, he walked on the water to go to Jesus."* (Matthew 14:28-29).

[59] *"And I also say to you that you are Peter, and on this rock I will build My church, and the gates of Hades shall not prevail against it."* (Matthew 16:18).

off, denying Jesus three times.[60] Oh, the shame he felt afterward, evidenced by his crying at the rooster's crow!

When the disciples saw Jesus on the shore after His resurrection, it was Peter who jumped into the water to head for shore when the rest brought in the boat[61] and it was Peter who hauled in the huge catch of fish.[62] Peter was still trying to demonstrate his devotion.

But Jesus shows us a more important principle. With three simple questions Jesus engaged Peter and enabled him to express his devotion while teaching him that achievement is not what matters most. Jesus asks Peter if he loved Him three times on that shore, and when Peter replied, "Yes," Jesus issued instructions that gave Peter the opportunity to express his love in a practical way.[63]

---

[60] *Now Peter sat outside in the courtyard. And a servant girl came to him, saying, "You also were with Jesus of Galilee." But he denied it before **them** all, saying, "I do not know what you are saying." And when he had gone out to the gateway, another **girl** saw him and said to those who were there, "This **fellow** also was with Jesus of Nazareth." But again he denied with an oath, "I do not know the Man!" And a little later those who stood by came up and said to Peter, "Surely you also are **one** of them, for your speech betrays you." Then he began to curse and swear, **saying**, "I do not know the Man!" Immediately a rooster crowed. And Peter remembered the word of Jesus who had said to him, "Before the rooster crows, you will deny Me three times." So he went out and wept bitterly* (Matthew 26:69-75).

[61] *Therefore that disciple whom Jesus loved said to Peter, "It is the Lord!" Now when Simon Peter heard that it was the Lord, he put on **his** outer garment (for he had removed it), and plunged into the sea* (John 21:7).

[62] *Simon Peter went up and dragged the net to land, full of large fish, one hundred and fifty-three; and although there were so many, the net was not broken* (John 21:11).

[63] *So when they had eaten breakfast, Jesus said to Simon Peter, "Simon, **son** of Jonah, do you love Me more than these?" He said to Him, "Yes, Lord; You know that I love You." He said to him, "Feed My lambs." He said to him again a second time, "Simon, **son** of Jonah, do you love Me?" He said to Him, "Yes, Lord; You know that I love You." He said to him, "Tend My sheep." He...*

A proud or perfectionist Peter might have carried out the ministry, but a broken Peter carried it out with compassion[64] and courage.[65]

How Judgment Propagates Shame: Releasing Celebrities from the Burden of Expectation

We can propagate the tendency in our society to honour achievement rather than character, or we can move our society forward by modelling a shift in thinking.

How do we view our heroes? Consider a particular person you admire: is it for who they are, for what they look like or for what they do that you admire them? In the intensely celebrity-focused culture we live in today, do we have a personal relationship with our heroes—those people we most admire? Or are they strangers? And if strangers, why is it that we want to model our lives after theirs? What is it about them that we find attractive, and how is that quality of substantial value to us? As we consider our heroes, what does our interest in them say about us? And in light of our desire to overcome insecurity, will the attributes we admire in others bring us closer to a positive self-image, or do we need to change our heroes in order to release ourselves from unhealthy attractions?

---

*...said to him the third time, "Simon, **son** of Jonah, do you love Me?" Peter was grieved because He said to him the third time, "Do you love Me?" And he said to Him, "Lord, You know all things; You know that I love You." Jesus said to him, "Feed My sheep" (John 21:15-17).*

64 *Then Peter said, "Silver and gold I do not have, but what I do have I give you: In the name of Jesus Christ of Nazareth, rise up and walk"* (Acts 3:6).

65 *So when Peter saw **it**, he responded to the people: "Men of Israel, why do you marvel at this?...To you first, God, having raised up His Servant Jesus, sent Him to bless you, in turning away every one **of you** from your iniquities"* (Acts 3:12-26).

Can we begin to release celebrities from judgment and curiosity? Just as we can rate ourselves with an invisible measuring rod for success, so we can do it to others. The media does it to our celebrities when it gossips, compares and shames them for their work or behaviour. The media looks at the external, and if we enter into that, are we not propagating the tendency in our society to look at achievement rather than at character?

Shall we admire others based on their personality, character or perhaps sense of humour? Can we influence commercialism that sees mentors and heroes only as images, objects and spectacles in magazines or on television, rather than as flesh-and-blood human beings? If our desire is for future generations to remember us for our character and not for our achievements, then let's hope and actively encourage the same for others.

God thinks about us in terms of who we are on the inside. He looks into motives, true intentions. He does not seek to deny us our needs or our desires[66] but develops our character first.[67]

Summary

Society tends to value people based on what they do rather than on what interests or motivates them.

God values our character above our achievements.

Respect for process and experience brings security. A successful outcome (or output) does not.

Does our view of celebrity propagate or transform our society's view? Do we look at output or character in our heroes?

---

[66] *Delight yourself also in the LORD, And He shall give you the desires of your heart* (Psalm 37:4).

[67] *And the LORD restored Job's losses when he prayed for his friends...So Job died, old and full of days* (Job 42:10-17).

Scriptures

> "*No mention shall be made of coral or quartz, For the price of wisdom **is** above rubies*" (Job 28:18).

> *For we dare not class ourselves or compare ourselves with those who commend themselves. But they, measuring themselves by themselves, and comparing themselves among themselves, are not wise* (2 Corinthians 10:12).

Chapter 6

Activating Change: Shifting Our Mindset from Product to Process

We will live in security as we match ourselves to who we were originally designed to be and as we recognize that the process of living life is inherently more valuable than the product we yield in our lifetime.

Inner Versus Outer Beauty

I'd like to take a moment to reflect on the truth that God looks at our hearts. As we get our hearts right with Him, we will be free from our self-imposed burden of achievement. This is what I mean by "inner beauty." God has designed us and knows how we are made. When we are aligned to that design, we have inner peace.

I used to say that my tombstone would read "She meant well." In spite of my inherent clumsiness with people, I aspire to be genuine, encouraging and thoughtful, never intentionally causing offence. Instead, I could be motivated by selfish interests, concerned with how someone else's perception of me will work to my advantage. I could play at being the perfect neighbour. If my motives are self-seeking, my behaviour might fool others, but it will never fool me, or God. My self-esteem will be directly proportionate to how much the person I project is the true representation of who I am on the inside.

We must first look at our hearts, not our behaviour, to find our self-worth. His plan is to unveil for us our true selves, if we will allow Him. Neither by penance nor by good deeds can we improve on God's masterpiece. And actually, if we allow ourselves to receive the full implication of this, we will realize that even if we sit on our proverbial behinds for the rest of our lives we will still be loved and accepted by God.

God sees us "sans disguise," and we are acceptable to Him because He made us and knows what He has crafted. To qualify, as we surrender to God we will be transformed, our "horrible nature" will be changed through the power of His Holy Spirit and we will become more and more like the person He created. We have been created in God's image. As we are being transformed into that which He intended so we are becoming more like Him.[68] On the one hand this is a supernatural process and comes only by way of faith, love and surrender. It is prideful and futile to try to gain anything by way of our own effort. It is pointless to put anyone but Jesus above us. Only He has real authority over us.[69] Grace is a great leveller; there is no need to feel inferior when we recognize that we are all equal in God's eyes.

On the other hand, I personally believe that each of us has a unique identity. God has created each of us as individuals. I believe when I was conceived something miraculous occured making me like no one else. I haven't a theological argument for this, but I believe each of us is an original design. As layers of insecurity, disillusionment and pain are peeled away, that design surfaces.

---

[68] *I beseech you therefore, brethren, by the mercies of God, that you present your bodies a living sacrifice, holy, acceptable to God, **which** is your reasonable service. And do not be conformed to this world, but be transformed by the renewing of your mind, that you may prove what **is** that good and acceptable and perfect will of God* (Romans 12:1-2).

[69] *And Jesus came and spoke to them, saying, "All authority has been given to Me in heaven and on earth"* (Matthew 28:18).

Teaching Our Children

Most of us were raised by parents who encouraged good behaviour and corrected bad. We were born knowing right from wrong, truth from lie.[70] When we live life truthfully, we will have peace with God (and ourselves). Part of our security is in the realization that we can do nothing to earn God's love.[71] Once we have received Jesus and made the commitment to follow Him, we have access to the security—the inner confidence—available through Him. We do not have to achieve to win God's love.

Seldom are we told this directly, seldom encouraged it by our parents, and our pride within will struggle against the concept that our deeds are in themselves empty and vain. Our pride would prefer us to revel in our successes as we pull ourselves up by our bootstraps. Success, we believe, will heal our secret shame.

I believe we are all fully aware of our inadequacies, our misguided thoughts and our sin. Taught it or not, deep down we know that "*all...fall short of the glory of God.*"[72] We all know shame. From an early age we see a child hiding his mistakes: the invisible friend broke the vase. She categorically denies eating chocolate (when her mouth is covered in it)! My little boy used to say, "I know" defensively, but when asked to demonstrate his understanding, he couldn't. Pride had already encouraged him to hide his ignorance, although he wasn't yet four years old.

---

[70] *For the wrath of God is revealed from heaven against all ungodliness and unrighteousness of men, who suppress the truth in unrighteousness, because what may be known of God is manifest in them...who exchanged the truth of God for the lie, and worshiped and served the creature rather than the Creator, who is blessed forever. Amen* (Romans 1:18-25).

[71] *For by grace you have been saved through faith, and that not of yourselves; **it is** the gift of God* (Ephesians 2:8).

[72] *...For all have sinned and fall short of the glory of God* (Romans 3:23).

When a child recognizes that he is flawed and is accepted in spite of those flaws, he can then explore who he is and learn that this is more significant than what he does. How do we raise our children: aren't they scolded or punished for what they do wrong, praised and rewarded for good behaviour? There seems to be no better way to teach them, and yet it places importance on their behaviour rather than on their hearts—their motives and attitudes.

Behaviour Separated from Motive

From a young age children learn they are judged on their behaviour rather than on who they are. There are several weaknesses with this. If we focus on behaviour as the measurement for growth, we train a child to understand that this is what is valued. But behaviour is more superficial than motive, and, while easier to grade, is less important. Instead, if we help them to know their hearts, children will discover a depth of self-awareness that will help them evaluate their actions as well as to know who they are and perhaps escape the treadmill of achievement altogether.

If we punish or reward a child for her behaviour, she learns only about acceptable behaviour. Instead, let's encourage children to explore their motives and challenge these motives if they are wrong. They will more quickly come to discover their need for a saviour. And in the times when their motive is pure, they will enjoy peace of mind. Having a positive self-image overall, irrespective of their outward behaviour, will yield unshakable confidence in the long run. As they grow up they will receive praise and discipline through their experiences, accomplishments and lessons, as they move from one state of glory to the next. Ultimately, our children can learn to love and share out of a love for others, rather than out of a fear of rejection or punishment.

We've established that if we learn to find value in our successes, it opens the door for our failures to bring us low and miserable.

Instead we want self-image to be positive whether we "win" or "lose." If children learn that pain is only a negative experience, they will not realize that pain can be a good instructor. If we train our children to find contentment in all circumstances, then suffering may not necessarily lead to dismay or a sense of failure, but rather it will signal an opportunity to grow.

Motivated by Love

If we don't have to "do" anything in order to feel good about ourselves, then why bother to do anything at all? It is not recommended that we sit on our posteriors indefinitely, because of the side effects of boredom, idle hands[73] and wasted talent, as well as disobedience to our call to obey.[74] Motivated by love rather than a need to achieve or to be accepted, our actions will become more productive. Our self-image will blossom because the experience of giving is life-fulfilling, we will have more success in our interpersonal relationships because others will realize our sincerity. While it may stretch us to believe it now, we can expect to have more joy and more fun in the process of our doing, knowing *"faith is the substance of things hoped for, the evidence of things not seen."*[75] All this results when we *do* because we want to, not because we ought to.

What If I Fail?

There is no failure if one truly believes that with experience comes growth. Growth is the measuring stick for success. It is

---

[73] *Because of laziness the building decays, And through idleness of hands the house leaks* (Ecclesiastes 10:18).

[74] *But be doers of the word, and not hearers only, deceiving yourselves* (James 1:22).

[75] Hebrews 11:1.

neither easy nor pain-free. But out of growth come satisfaction, excitement and joy. Our love won't always be accepted, but if we are generous or kind to others out of a love for them and for God, rather than out of angst or fear, we will find strength and self-acceptance that builds us up.

Growing: the Process of Becoming

Psalm 139:1–6 reveals that our inner being is defined and known by God. Matthew 10:30 reinforces that God has created each of us and knows us intimately. Through our journey with Him, we can discover our true character even after socialization and experience has corrupted it. The closer we become to the person we were created to be, the more secure and peaceful we will be.

> *O LORD, You have searched me and known **me**. You know my sitting down and my rising up; You understand my thought afar off. You comprehend my path and my lying down, And are acquainted with all my ways. For **there** is not a word on my tongue, But behold, O LORD, You know it altogether. You have hedged me behind and before, And laid Your hand upon me. **Such** knowledge is too wonderful for me; It is high, I cannot **attain** it.*[76]

Also, "*...the very hairs of your head are all numbered.*"[77] God knows us better than we know ourselves. If He, the creator who is all-knowing, is willing to accept us for who we are, who are we to argue?

God will not ignore our mistakes, but He will use them to teach us and to enable us to grow. Growth always yields inner satisfaction, even though at times meeting the challenges along the

---

[76] Psalm 139:1-6.

[77] Matthew 10:30.

way can be uncomfortable. Witness the child struggling to ride a bicycle or the teen learning new math. The victory is always worth the effort, and the joy in learning brings celebration.

Living Comfortably with Ourselves

Originally, the title I chose for this chapter was "When We Make Mistakes."

Mistakes are inevitable. But when we accept fully the grace of God and let that understanding seep into our psyche, we find that it becomes easier to admit our mistakes. We can know that we are doing our best at this moment and we are right where we are supposed to be. Someone with a healthy perspective releases a prayer something like this: "God, I made (another) mistake; I'm sorry."

It's profoundly simple. The focus is on the person affected by the mistake, and our responsibility is taken for it. By going directly to God, telling Him how we feel and asking Him to forgive the mistake, we can receive His forgiveness and move on. As we believe in God, we can also trust the God who promises His love.

Sometimes, we must also make a direct apology to the person we've wronged. This is not to be mistaken for taking responsibility for someone else's mistakes, but we do need to make restitution to those we have wronged through our ignorance, negligence or own deliberate fault. When we do that, irrespective of their response to us, we can put it behind us.

Another way to go to God directly to ask forgiveness is to have another person alongside you who is trustworthy and more experienced in prayer. You can talk over your regret and any fears with this person, thank him for listening, and pray together. I urge you to resist any temptation to ask his opinion though, as it may be a temptation to seek approval. Instead, trust your own conscience and the inner work God is doing in you through your sincere confession and prayer. By sharing with someone else you can enjoy getting the issue off your chest. Then it's important to move on. By telling rather than hiding a conviction, you have exposed it. Truth sets us free.

Finally, our minds hold a minefield of opportunity for the father of lies[78] to perpetuate self-doubt and condemnation. Sometimes, when the mind is fighting really hard to shout negativity and fear at us, it's all we can do to hold on to this Scripture: "*There is therefore now no condemnation to those who are in Christ Jesus.*"[79] You can trust this as you move on after repentance. If you sense an accusation upon you, it is not from God. But if a word of correction resonates within you, it is something you will need to take to the Lord so that He can prune that which needs to be changed within you.

Perfection Is God's Job, Not Ours

"*You, therefore, must be perfect, as your heavenly Father is perfect.*"[80] In society today, with advertising and plastic surgery promoting the perfect body, face and look, our perspective on what is healthy self-perception has been completely lost. God is not talking about *perfect* physical beauty or even outward achievement in other areas, but in context He is talking about our hearts and our character. For our own good—for emotional health as well as physical, intellectual and spiritual well-being—we need to

---

[78] "*You are of **your** father the devil, and the desires of your father you want to do. He was a murderer from the beginning, and does not stand in the truth, because there is no truth in him. When he speaks a lie, he speaks from his own **resources**, for he is a liar and the father of it*" (John 8:44).

[79] ***There** is therefore now no condemnation to those who are in Christ Jesus, who do not walk according to the flesh, but according to the Spirit* (Romans 8:1).

[80] Matthew 5:48, RSV.

reach for the goal of perfection, always knowing that He is the author and finisher of our faith.[81] Though we may not reach a state of perfection this side of the grave, we can do our best and leave the rest to Him. This attitude will enable us to be free from comparison to others, free from perfectionism and free from fear of failure.

Summary

Our culture says that our identity is in what we do, but God identifies us by who we are internally rather than by our career or activity.

Mistakes are learning opportunities for growth when we admit them, learn from them and move on.

We may not be perfect, but we can be free knowing that where we are is right where God wants us to be.

Scriptures

I do not understand my own actions. For I do not do what I want, but I do the very thing I hate (Romans 7:15, RSV).

*…One thing I **do**, forgetting those things which are behind and reaching forward to those things which are ahead, I press toward the goal for the prize of the upward call of God in Christ Jesus* (Philippians 3:13b-14).

I can do all things through Christ who strengthens me (Philippians 4:13).

---

[81] *Looking unto Jesus, the author and finisher of **our** faith, who for the joy that was set before Him endured the cross, despising the shame, and has sat down at the right hand of the throne of God* (Hebrews 12:2).

Chapter 7

Unconditional Love: Trusting God's and Taking Time to Develop Our Own

Security rests in our being accepted and loved. God loves us unconditionally. Patiently, He waits for us to acknowledge Him, then He gently teaches us through His Holy Spirit and watches us as we crawl, stumble, stand…and fall from time to time, each step taking us a little closer to the pure soul He created us to be. *Unconditional* is defined as "not limited by our conditions; absolute; unreserved."[82] Knowing we are loved unconditionally strengthens us, giving us the security and space to grow that we need.

But knowing we are loved is only the first step. To mature, we need to give love. And as we give, so we will receive. The healthier is the love we give, the healthier will be what is returned to us. By healthy, I mean pure, without conditions, expectations, neediness or demands.

Loving Unconditionally

Through our giving of love, there is *power* to conquer the thoughts that are full of fear and self-doubt. As we sow, so shall we reap; by loving, we will be loved. As we focus on *giving* love, we are

---

[82] *The New Webster Encylopedic Dictionary of the English Language,* s.v. "unconditional."

less apt to be preoccupied with ourselves and the fear of being unloved. By focusing our attention outward we are less apt to be critical, and less exposed to criticism as well.

Take for example, romantic love and its power over our thoughts and feelings. When we first "fall in love," our focus is on the other person entirely, enjoying all the excitement and thrill of being in love. Although this love may be superficial or temporary, it is intense, all consuming. When it is reciprocated, there is the hope that it will grow into a permanent relationship. But that first phase of infatuation is "blind" to any fault and totally enthralling, focused toward the other person. How many of us have been so infatuated that we see no fault in our *amour* or find their "odd quirk" adorable or charming (often to find it an annoying habit after matrimony!)?

Imagine now God's unconditional love. He sees our faults plainly *but by his grace it is as though they are unseen,* and He loves us regardless. Let us receive that love, and the power that comes with it, as we grow in confidence and assurance.

When we see how Jesus loves, through the countless stories in the Gospels,[83] we also see God's love.[84] Universally, Jesus has been accepted as a brilliant teacher and role model for loving others; as we follow His model, loving Him and others, we focus outwardly and imitate the best giver of love. Furthermore, as He is the Son of God and very much alive, we also experience our love's return as we engage with Him, learning from the Master of love.

This kind of love is not a feeling, but rather it is a decision, a choice. For the Christian, to love is not an option; to love even when we may not "feel" like it is an act of obedience. We are

---

[83] The books of Matthew, Mark, Luke and John.

[84] "*I and **My** Father are one*" (John 10:30).

commanded to "*love one another,*"[85] i.e., other believers, and in an act of love we "*Go therefore and make disciples of all the nations, baptizing them in the name of the Father and of the Son and of the Holy Spirit.*"[86] We are commissioned to love humanity from all nations, in the hope that through us they will recognize Jesus and receive the same salvation we have received. Thank goodness the power of the Holy Spirit gives us love to pour out when we seem to lack the capacity ourselves!

Why Love?

Humanity, both believers and non-believers, need to be loved. Studies have shown that infants in over-crowded orphanages, untouched and unloved, die. Love, though intangible, is as basic a human need as food and water. It is how we have been designed.

What Is Love?

"*It is more blessed to give than to receive*" (Acts 20:35). How we receive love is by giving a quality of love that is defined as follows:

> *Love suffers long **and** is kind; love does not envy; love does not parade itself, is not puffed up; does not behave rudely, does not seek its own, is not provoked, thinks no evil; does not rejoice in iniquity, but rejoices in the truth; bears all things, believes all things, hopes all things, endures all things. Love never fails.*[87]

To be enabled to love in this way requires the Holy Spirit, who equips us when we step out in faith and seek to do His will.

---

[85] "*This is My commandment, that you love one another as I have loved you*" (John 15:12).

[86] Matthew 28:19.

[87] 1 Corinthians 13:4-8a.

Agape commonly refers to God's unconditional love. At its essence, it is the unconditional love that gives and asks for nothing in return. This love gives and wants the best for others. It does not focus on self. When we give this love, we make room for others in our minds. We also build relationships.

As we receive unconditional love from God and from our brothers and sisters in Christ, we experience that our acceptance has no conditions. Our perspective becomes elevated above our fear of rejection, and the hurtful actions or attitudes of others become powerless against our sense of self-worth. Our love is not limited by others' unloving behaviour toward us. In relationship, when we reach this level of love, we rest secure in our own conscience and have peace with God, knowing that we have given and done our best to nurture, encourage and accept others for who they are in the same way we long to be loved, encouraged and accepted.

Jesus: the Perfect Role Model

Jesus was the perfect role model, and to attain His level of love we need His Holy Spirit. Fallen humanity on its own lacks the selflessness of unconditional love, but through Christ all things are possible.[88] The Holy Spirit will give us the ability to love as we are called to love. So we needn't burden ourselves with the notion we "should" love in this way. Don't say to yourself, "I must achieve this standard of loving or I'm a failure." Instead, have the attitude to surrender to the Holy Spirit, asking for His ability to love in this way. As you surrender daily to His will, He will lead you to loving as He loves through you.

---

[88] *I can do all things through Christ who strengthens me* (Philippians 4:13).

Love in Action

How do we demonstrate this *agape* love?

First I ask myself, "How would I like to be loved?" and then I seek to do that. Jesus said love does unto others as we would have them do to us and that we must turn the other cheek.[89]

Speaking practically, we can try to get to know someone, his likes and dislikes, and take those into account when interacting with him. Ask questions. Discover where he comes from and what he values. Be genuinely interested in who he is and what is important to him. Encourage him when he is feeling down, help him when he is in need, respect him for who he is, and above all, accept him.[90] These are human strategies to gain a conscious understanding of someone else and to show him love in a way that will benefit and encourage him. The emphasis is on him, and not on us.

One thing I've learned very recently is that folks who appear confident and easygoing can be quite sensitive, needing to receive respect or acknowledgement from me. I've discovered that just as I am much more sensitive than I appear, so are others. Applying my newfound awareness, I'm learning to listen better and to defer to others in conversation, paying a high regard for what they have to say. I've discovered that people like to be heard, just as I do, and as I view them with compassion, I enjoy what they have to say more than I used to. I hope this will build encouragement and respect in others when they are around me.

---

[89] "*To him who strikes you on the **one** cheek, offer the other also. And from him who takes away your cloak, do not withhold **your** tunic either…And just as you want men to do to you, you also do to them likewise*" (Luke 6:29-31).

[90] Parable of the Good Samaritan (Luke 10:29-37)

Unconditionally Loved

Choosing *genuinely* to accept others as they are, looking for and encouraging good things in them, and praying particularly for those you dislike—these are ways of demonstrating love. And while the motive is not to receive but to give, you will discover that such will be returned to you, *"pressed down, shaken together, and running over."*[91]

"The things which you learned and received and heard and saw in me, these do, and the God of peace will be with you."[92] God has shown His unconditional love to you as you have read these pages and processed many of the Scriptures given. When we give out what we have received from God, we sustain what we have already received and increase its measure. By practicing, we improve. Consider the budding pianist. First he may be inspired when he hears a brilliant composition played; he may decide he wants to play like that. The accomplished performer may sit by him, coach him, help him to improve; but ultimately he needs to practice in order to play well. It is in the practice that he grows to achieve his aspirations.

Likewise, in order to grow in our capacity to love, we need not only the power of the Holy Spirit but also our own co-operative effort with Him to grow in our ability to love.

On the other side of the coin, we also need to be aware of and to avoid negative encounters. In order to grow in a healthy way, to stay away from our insecurity for good, there are temptations we are meant to avoid.

---

[91] *"Give, and it will be given to you: good measure, pressed down, shaken together, and running over will be put into your bosom. For with the same measure that you use, it will be measured back to you"* (Luke 6:38).

[92] Philippians 4:9.

First, beware: *"Judge not, that you be not judged,"*[93] for when judgment sets in we judge others by our own standards, and that will prompt them to judge us by theirs. That can start to foster insecurity all over again.

With wisdom comes self-awareness and the acknowledging of your underlying motives for relationship. I'd like to take a moment to warn you: please, please, *please*, do not do what I did in my early days as a believer. In those days, with great enthusiasm but still full of insecurity, I went forth blindly, throwing myself into relationships (particularly romantic ones), with my heart on my sleeve, eager to give unconditional love indiscriminately and naively. I believed it would be returned. Cloaked in sincerity but ignorance, I still loved out of my insecure need for love.

There is always the risk of rejection because of the other person's issues. Do not believe you cannot get hurt. It is healthier—and emotionally safer—to recognize the risk,[94] the hurt, and to rest in God, who enables us to overcome the pain of rejection. Then as you grow in the healing you've received you will be better equipped to give to a wider variety of people.

Fear of Criticism

You have overcome the fear of what others will say or think of you! As you meditate on God's promises and trust in God's love, wait patiently for the fulfilment. He knows your need for relationship and will supply you with flesh-and-blood friendships that will build you up, challenge you to mature and give you joyful moments to enjoy together. Give yourself time to adjust and time to grow.

---

[93] Matthew 7:1.

[94] *"For which of you, intending to build a tower, does not sit down first and count the cost, whether he has **enough** to finish **it**"* (Luke 14:28).

Giving indiscriminately at first may well be a striving "to get," albeit in a subtle way, in order to fill a void. It will surely mangle your already delicate, sensitive healing ego. That is what happened to me at first. I recommend a different path: to patiently and thoughtfully consider how God might lead you, by His wisdom and strength, to those to whom you can give and not expect anything in return. Children, the infirm, and the handicapped, for example, need comfort and company. Yet in the role of caregiver, you may more easily stem the urge to find emotional comfort from them. Then, gradually, as you apply and grow, receiving His assurance and divine protection along the way, you will be propelled further toward Christ's character. As His ability to love grows in you, you will find that the sense of security you have been seeking is strengthening, and you will be ready to engage others who have less love to offer themselves.

Summary

God's unconditional love teaches us how to love unconditionally.

Focusing on others builds our own self-esteem and ability to give and to receive love.

We have no option but to love.

Love is that which seeks to benefit another and not ourselves. It is focused outward.

Practise makes perfect, literally.

What goes around comes around, be it love or judgment.

No need to dive in! Taking baby steps God's way is best.

Scripture

> *Beloved, let us love one another, for love is of God; and everyone who loves is born of God and knows God. He who does not love does not know God, for God is love. In this the love of God was manifested toward us, that God has sent His only begotten Son into the world, that we might live through Him. In this is love, not that we loved God, but that He loved us and sent His Son to **be** the propitiation for our sins. Beloved, if God so loved us, we also ought to love one another. No one has seen God at any time. If we love one another, God abides in us, and His love has been perfected in us. By this we know that we abide in Him, and He in us, because He has given us of His Spirit* (1 John 4:7-13).

Summary to date

To find emotional security the following revelations can renew your current mindset and take you toward your goal:

- God is totally sovereign. If we believe that and live it we will not fear our circumstances or people's opinions of us.
- God is love. If we receive this—and His love—our sense of security is sure.
- God loves us for who we are, not what we are or do. When we have faith in Jesus' resurrection and sonship and commit to following Him, we receive God's Holy Spirit, who empowers us to love as He loves us. It is in this that true and lasting security exists.

Scripture

> *"A new commandment I give to you, that you love one another; as I have loved you, that you also love one another. By this all will know that you are My disciples, if you have love for one another"* (John 13:34-35).

105

Becoming Free

Applying Scripture to the Healing Process

Chapter 8

Trust and Sound Judgment: Recognizing People of Character, Building on Our Own

"*The way of a fool is right in his own eyes, but a wise man listens to advice.*"[95] "*The fear of man lays a snare, but he who trusts in the LORD is safe,*"[96]

Now that we have found peace within, we can begin to relax into our new self-confidence and shift our focus of attention from ourselves to others. But to whom will we entrust our newly found, perhaps fragile, inner peace? Giving and encouraging acceptance toward others enables us to express good-will and keeps our attention away from ourselves; it's also very likely that we will end up receiving more than we give (although this is not the motive for doing it)!

Important to our healing process is to focus outward and to surround ourselves with people who will bolster our confidence in a meaningful way. How can we discern the relationships that will build us up? All of us need friends. But there will be friendships that will inspire our courage and bolster our confidence. Some will do so by their positive words to us. But even more importantly, some will build us by their need. As we look outward, we will see all kinds of people who are in need—elderly, children, homeless

---

95 Proverbs 12:15, RSV.

96 Proverbs 29:25, RSV.

and the infirm are obvious people with needs. Charity work is admirable and fulfilling. In day-to-day contact there are those to whom we can give.

Giving

If we can learn to take a step back from ourselves when we are with others, we can better see who the other person is. By listening to others and focusing on their interests and needs, we can discover our competence and, by encouraging them, feel good about ourselves. By giving rather than receiving attention, we will discover our strengths and others' vulnerability and recognize that our humanity is really quite the same as everyone else's. In learning this firsthand, we gain perspective, make new friendships and build our self-respect and self-image, while we've helped someone else in the process. It really is a win-win situation.

Life is dynamic, and we have no control over others or events as a whole. Invariably, both trying times and times of celebration will come and go. Such is the ebb and flow of life. Some experiences will be testing, and we can choose to see these tests as opportunities rather than threats. If we do that, our burden will be lighter.

I still have to check myself, from time to time, when conflict with others rears itself. Often I automatically fear the worst, rejection, when in fact the strain is usually a result of miscommunication. To trust and take people at face value is still something I occasionally need to remind myself of.

At the core of our healing is *our attitude*. In our journey this is what we have control over. We can't control others or God, but we can control our attitude to the people we meet and the circumstances God puts us in.

Our Attitude Determines Our Experience

The most important relationship we can foster is our relationship with the giver of life, love and security—our God. But there is a natural human need for human contact. When the quality of human contact seems too limited, look up and see: God is there to comfort and to guide, to surround us with encouragement.

In addition, to be part of a fellowship is vital if we are to grow in our knowledge and experience of Him, yet so often people have said Christians have let them down. Finding and nurturing relationships with brothers and sisters in Christ has no substitute, as these relationships have at their centre the Jesus who models and gives agape, the unconditional love that we all need.

When our relationship with Him is strong but we have limited human contact, ask Him why. What is His purpose in putting us into this solitary position? When we trust that the situation exists for our benefit, we can accept and enjoy the privacy! There have been times in my life when I've longed for a close friend but had none. I don't think I'm particularly off-putting, so there has to be a higher reason. In those times I've always discovered that it was meant to be a season for reflection.

Have you ever noticed that when you are busy you don't miss companionship nearly as much as when the day is empty of tasks and chores and you have time on your hands? We can be so engrossed in our own needs and timetables that we don't see others. Yet, when we have time, do we make the best use of it? Do we give when we can, to balance the occasions when we've little time for others? There are always those with more needs than we have, always. So, *"give, and it will be given to you; good measure, pressed down, shaken together, running over, will be put into your lap. For the measure you give will be the measure you get back."*[97]

---

[97] Luke 6:38, RSV.

111

Antenna and Choices

When there are a lot of people around us, with whom do we choose to *build* relationships? How do we distinguish between those who will be an encouragement and those who will not, those who will accept and engage with us and those who will not? My answers may not be profound, but I trust they are sound

First, we can respond to those who show an interest in us. We need to look away from ourselves and to them. Years ago, a famous film director and star had been loosely quoted as saying, "I don't want to go to a party where I'm invited." Often due to a poor self-image we have sought out friendships with those we esteem as greater than ourselves. Rather, if we appreciate those who appreciate us, we can begin to build through mutual respect.

As we reach out to build new relationships, let's not let our self-image be tied to success or failure. It is important that we learn not to take personally those who seem to reject our hand of friendship.

Where a person comes from—his birthplace, his economic family history, his education—will influence who he is personally. As we reach out, taking an interest in a person's background can not only show that we acknowledge them, but it gives us a topic for conversation. And while we gain some degree of insight into his priorities, culture and even character, it can also help us to discover areas of compatibility.

Time

There might be no better way, in our society of fast pace and busyness, to show our appreciation, to demonstrate generosity and care, than by *giving our time* to another person.[98]

---

[98] Gary Chapman, PhD, *Love As a Way of Life* (London: Hodder & Stoughton, 2008), 136.

While I've already suggested that we can listen and encourage, secondly I'd like to suggest that we can *take time* to establish budding relationships: time to see the other person; time to assess their values and needs; then, time to share ours. And as those relationships become established, we might find they begin to transform: some may deepen, some may strengthen, and some unfortunately may fall away.

Temper

Perhaps like me, you have a tendency to be temperamental. Freedom does not imply a lack of self-control or courtesy. In fact, as we move in greater freedom we will be more responsible than ever before for our attitude and behaviour toward others.

Guarding the Tongue

"There is one whose rash words are like sword thrusts, but the tongue of the wise brings healing."[99] If our habit is to speak our minds based on our emotions, we will benefit from learning to *guard what we say* in our circumstances, our relationships and ourselves. *"The tongue is a fire,"*[100] and as we learn to guard our words we will protect ourselves—and others—against negativity, fear and anxiety, in which we might otherwise get caught. What we say has power, to heal or to harm, so we need to be alert to what pours from our lips. I try to consider before speaking: "Is what I am about to say life-giving?" If it's not, I try to keep it to myself.

I am still on a learning curve. As an impulsive person, learning to hold my tongue when I want to burst out a response to a situation that seems unjust has never been easy for me, but as I look at

---

[99] Proverbs 12:18, RSV.

[100] James 3:6a.

the other person's perspective and remind myself that others are not out to hurt me, I can go beyond a knee-jerk reaction and aim for a gracious response rather than a hot reaction.

When we are tempted to react to a situation, we would do well to learn that *reaction* and *response* are not one and the same. To react means to take what has been presented and take emotional "action." We have *re*ceived, and so we act; in other words, we "*react*." On the other hand, to respond is to consider, to "ponder" what has been presented and reply to it, perhaps with a measured response. Reaction is by its nature lacking in self-control, while response is considered and requires at least some self-control as one takes time to formulate a reply.

Some biblical evidence for this council is as follows: "*But they who wait for the LORD shall renew their strength, they shall mount up with wings like eagles, they shall run and not be weary, they shall walk and not faint.*"[101]

Success comes through waiting: "*For God did not give us a spirit of timidity but a spirit of power and love and self-control*"[102] advocates self-control.

"*But the fruit of the Spirit is love, joy, peace, patience, kindness, goodness, faithfulness, gentleness, self-control.*"[103] When we consider the full weight of these fruit we recognize a peaceful calm that pervades as we meditate.

Developing Sincerity = Openness + Candour + Grace

You may have noticed that in looking outward, giving attention to others, *we have been growing in our own character.* The basic principle of *sowing and reaping* will echo through every aspect of

---

[101] Isaiah 40:31, RSV.

[102] 2 Timothy 1:7, RSV.

[103] Galatians 5:22-23, RSV.

our lives.[104] As we plant kindness, will we not reap? As we sow trust, we will identify others who are trustworthy, considerate and giving. To build healthy relationships we need to seek them out, offer ourselves and sometimes take a leap of faith in the person with whom we are building a friendship.

I have a formula: Sincerity (S) = Openness (O) + Candour (C) + Grace (G). When I want a truthful, warm relationship I need first to be truthful and warm—this is how I define *openness*. Should the other person respond in kind, this will give us an opportunity to deepen our communication. I believe that in a deep and honest relationship there will come a time when *candour* is necessary. Honesty is not licence to be rude, but, sprinkled with *grace*—that gift of giving more goodness, patience, generosity and acceptance than is deserved—any comment can be made palatable. Speak as we would wish to be spoken to, and we can perhaps find in ourselves tact and kindness.

As we develop the ability to contain our anger at emotional times, we will learn to be honest without attacking. As we learn grace and practice forgiveness, we will be able to be candid without being condemning. Sincerity with love is a life-giving trait, one that builds up esteem and engenders good-will and respect. Isn't it how we long to be treated?[105] And as we respond to others in this way, we will engender the same response. Notice that our focus has completely shifted from concern for our needs to awareness of those of others. This is a sign of good character in a secure person.

---

[104] *He who sows sparingly will also reap sparingly, and he who sows bountifully will also reap bountifully* (2 Corinthians 9:6). *Do not be deceived, God is not mocked; for whatever a man sows, that he will also reap. For he who sows to his flesh will of the flesh reap corruption, but he who sows to the Spirit will of the Spirit reap everlasting life. And let us not grow weary while doing good, for in due season we shall reap if we do not lose heart.* (Galatians 6:7-9).

[105] "*Therefore, whatever you want men to do to you, do also to them, for this is the Law and the Prophets*" (Matthew 7:12).

Remember Fear?

When apprehension lurks, remember that God is always with you. Pray to find perspective. And you don't have to move emotional mountains. Give yourself the same time and patience you are learning to express to others. Love yourself as you are learning to love others.

Combatting Panic

As creatures of habit, we can draw back into old styles of temperament and insecurity even when logic and our will want to move us forward. Human nature is such that we are comfortable with what is most familiar. So, emotional wholeness might be hard to get used to at first. I have a relative who calls feelings of discomfort "itchy"; we can actually feel a little *itchy with peace* if it is unusual to us. So it is important not to put a great deal of reliance on our feelings in the earliest stages of building security.

Challenges and difficult situations too can draw us into old habits of worry and insecurity. Don't be too hard on yourself if you feel "out of sorts" or take a step backward from time to time; we need to hope for the best and be prepared for disappointment and open to building relationships in a new way. Usually, transformation is a gradual process. We needn't strive for over-achievement, hurrying to the goal of self-confidence. Rather, let's have the freedom to grow at God's pace.

The Aspiration

"*I press toward the goal for the prize of the upward call of God in Christ Jesus*"[106] is inscribed on a poster that hangs in my kitchen. It is probably my favourite Scripture, because it reminds me that I have

---

[106] Philippians 3:14.

something good to reach for but I don't have to "be there" yet. When we walk with God, and our confidence is not in ourselves, nor in others, but in Him, we have the assurance, "*if God is for us, who can be against us?*"[107] We never fail with Him, but rather He just keeps giving us the same "test" until we pass! As we face one challenge after another, we receive more opportunity to grow. It is as though we're building "confidence" muscles. It's just like how we learned to ride a bicycle, as during that process we did invariably fall off.

A Word of Caution

Security in a vacuum, isolated and untested by relationship, is limited. So we need to build relationships. Perhaps in exploring new truly healthy relationships, it is wisest to seek people of character! We're used to shaky relationships founded on a level of dependence or stirred by a degree of insecurity. Now, let us build friendships, but for new purpose. Let's develop relationships that will be truthful, reciprocal, and built on mutual respect.

We need to look deeper than in the past at any opportunity of friendship, to consider whether it will help us to grow or will prevent us from maturing in our faith, confidence and self-worth. That could mean that some of our friendships will have to be suspended while we strengthen ourselves, or they may have to be radically transformed.

In the past, if at random we seized any source of friendship available, we may have developed some unhealthy ones. Though we are called to love all, not all of those we love are worthy of our trust. We will need wisdom and discernment to identify the character of those of our friends who will support us as we grow.

Sound judgment comes best from God and from using our common sense. Read the Book of Proverbs and you'll find dozens

---

[107] Romans 8:31b.

of relationship tips about those to embrace and those to avoid. For example, a look at Proverbs chapter 1 defines people of wisdom, while chapter 2 suggests those to avoid; Proverbs 10–15 describes the outcomes of good and poor behaviour; Proverbs 17:17 identifies the good friend from the false. It may sound obvious, but people who encourage us, support us and are positive will fit well with our growing security.

A Lesson in Compassion

Years ago, broken and devastated by the breakup of a romantic relationship, I visited a psychologist. I'm sure he was very able, if somewhat clinical. On that visit he told me in a formal and detached tone, while I was in tears and confusion, that I had poor judgment in choosing relationships. I thought I then showed good judgment in deciding to seek counsel elsewhere, from someone with more compassion and for a smaller fee than his $50 an hour (in 1983). But that didn't change the fact that the man was right. Though how he put it across was cold and less kind than it might have been, I had demonstrated poor judgment in my choice of "trusted friends" (perhaps in a counsellor as well). Information was not enough; nor was a listening ear. I needed counsel from someone who would build on my strengths, not only highlight my weaknesses.

Mutual trust and respect in friendship is both valuable and attainable. People who will tell you the (whole) truth can be trusted. Even though such friendships may be rare, and you may, on occasion, get hurt feelings, it is worth having friends worthy of your trust.[108]

---

[108] *Better is open rebuke than hidden love. Faithful are the wounds of a friend; profuse are the kisses of an enemy* (Proverbs 27:5-6, RSV).

Relationships to Suspend or Avoid

Early in the process to achieve emotional security, you may want to reduce contact with friends or relatives who make great emotional demands on you. If you are only learning how to say no, and a dear old friend is insistent, you can stand your ground and say you aren't ready to give more than you have, in time or emotional commitment. You might feel a little shaky afterward, but that will subside. Don't allow bitterness or hardheartedness to settle in; eventually you will be able to say no to demands without feeling anxious and without having to avoid those who make the demands, and you will be able to say "yes" without feeling overwhelmed, even to that demanding type who insist that their needs are greater than anyone else's. In other words, don't burn your bridges, terminating friendships that seem unloving or unwise. Never say never! Relationships change, people change, and good can come from almost any acquaintance.

I am married to a man with an astrological sign I had vowed I'd never date. If I'd stuck to such a foolish vow I'd have missed the last eighteen years of my life married to him. Instead, I repented of my prejudice.[109] I married and have shared a wonderful life with my spouse! (Thank you, Alan.)

There are some relationships, such as with your spouse or children, where you cannot reduce contact, even on a temporary basis. In those situations, be as open as you can about what you are learning, take full responsibility for yourself, ask for patience, and don't place expectations on them. You may be pleasantly surprised at their compassion, but don't expect them to alter their habits or dynamics for your benefit. Rather, see the relationships as part of your journey and part of the parameters in which you are to grow.

---

[109] God equates astrology to other sorcery and divination which are *"evil in the sight of the LORD."* (2 Chronicles 33:6b)

Co-dependency: Attractive but Unhealthy

Would you advise a young man to draw toward a woman who is lurking in the night? Similarly, a friendship built around neediness may seem comforting but is a danger to someone who is overcoming insecurity. Learning to be independent (rather than co-dependent) in your friendships can be lonely at times. But while some friends may sympathize and hold your hand and listen, it may not necessarily be healthy. Be aware that if your conversation is "me-centred" you might inadvertently be drawing yourself back into old habits of self-pity or self-condemnation and self-centredness, for the sake of complying with the other person's need to be needed.

Some people who listen and comfort are seeking to build you up, but others may be seeking to fulfil their own needs. Not every friend will be suitable for sharing your journey with. Those respectful of you won't press you to hang your heart with them all the time.

Ask God for discernment in your relationships, to reveal potential with people who are strong yet sensitive, confident in themselves and in relationships. The truth is that no one but Jesus is perfect. Jesus builds up our self-esteem tremendously as we relate to Him. But we are in this world and need to interact with others as well. Finding and sharing with people worthy of our trust and growing in maturity is valuable, albeit perhaps rare.

Brothers and Sisters of Faith

"*Unfaithful creatures! Do you not know that friendship with the world is enmity with God? Therefore whoever wishes to be a friend of the world makes himself an enemy of God.*"[110] Watchman Nee, an astute

---

[110] James 4:4, RSV.

teacher of God's Word, taught in the last century that to put your heart completely with that of an unbeliever was, in effect, to put God second.[111] Here is another consideration in choosing new relationships: do not be unequally yoked with an unbeliever.[112] If you place higher value on a relationship with an unbeliever than with Jesus, or with those who know Jesus, you will be constantly frustrated by the inability to communicate about what is central to your life. Love them, care for them, but don't expect complete reciprocity. They haven't got Jesus, so they simply haven't got it to give.

Expectations and Broken Relationships

Certain expectations are reasonable in a trusting friendship, so it hurts when people let us down. But don't be shocked if it happens, and don't retreat into fear and self-loathing. The oversight was probably not intentional. Inevitably, there will come a time when you will let a friend down too, without meaning to.

In both cases, try to discuss the disappointment with *sincere openness*. Lasting friendship endures the tough times, and the relationship can actually deepen as a result of working through a misunderstanding. A friendship cannot be forced, however. If the other person cannot discuss it with you, pray for strength for that person. If you have the opportunity, offer your acceptance of them, and wait. They may come round. Forgive them if they apologize, release them if they can't, and hope for reconciliation in due time. Then, *let it go*. Often, quite unexpectedly, God may send someone else to encourage you. What she has to say will build you up and

---

[111] Watchman Nee, *Do All to the Glory of God* (New York: Christian Fellowship Publishers, Inc., 1974), 109.

[112] *Do not be unequally yoked together with unbelievers. For what fellowship has righteousness with lawlessness? And what communion has light with darkness?* (2 Corinthians 6:14).

strengthen your hope and faith. Praise God for her, and bless her by graciously accepting the encouragement you need.

Knowing our Motive

In all things, we need to know our own hearts. To seek a relationship for gain, be it emotional or positional, will be unfulfilling. To know our need and to acknowledge it rather than judge it is wise, but to follow it will be empty. Giving for its own sake, rather, is pure and life-inspiring and will build our self-esteem. When we give only to get back, we will be disappointed and will miss the beauty and joy there is in the act of giving.

Building relationship has no formula. But by seeking to grow in character and learning to assess the character of others, you will discover trustworthy, loving, faithful and healthy people. Be kind to those weaker than yourself, but steer clear of relationships that draw you into feelings of inadequacy or dependency.

Summary

Guard your words as though they had power because they do![113]

Living with a sense of security means that we are not emotionally buffeted with each difficult relationship or challenging situation.

We will face a challenge repeatedly until we overcome it.

Security is found inside relationship; it cannot exist on its own. We all need friends.

Learning to trust our own judgment about others' character and capability gives us a greater sense of our own emotional security.

---

[113] Note: God created the world using words. Satan tempted with words. Words are powerful, so let us use words to speak life-giving messages.

Having a trustworthy friend does not mean you will never be hurt; it does mean you can grow together as you overcome disappointments through communication, mutual acceptance and Godly love.

Accept encouragement. Seek to give it too.

Scriptures

Give ear to my words, O LORD, Consider my meditation. Give heed to the voice of my cry, My King and my God, For to You I will pray. My voice You shall hear in the morning, O LORD; In the morning I will direct it to You, And I will look up. For You are not a God who takes pleasure in wickedness, Nor shall evil dwell with You. The boastful shall not stand in Your sight; You hate all workers of iniquity (Psalm 5:1-5).

Blessed is the man Who walks not in the counsel of the ungodly, Nor stands in the path of sinners, Nor sits in the seat of the scornful; But his delight is in the law of the LORD, And in His law he meditates day and night. He shall be like a tree Planted by the rivers of water, That brings forth its fruit in its season, Whose leaf also shall not wither; And whatever he does shall prosper. The ungodly are not so, But are like the chaff which the wind drives away. Therefore the ungodly shall not stand in the judgment, Nor sinners in the congregation of the righteous. For the LORD knows the way of the righteous, But the way of the ungodly shall perish (Psalm 1:1-6).

Behold, how good and how pleasant it is For brethren to dwell together in unity! It is like the precious oil upon the head, Running down on the beard, The beard of Aaron, Running down on the edge of his garments. It is like the dew of Hermon, Descending upon the mountains of Zion; For there the LORD commanded the blessing— Life forevermore (Psalm 133:1-3).

Chapter 9

God Is Love: Walking in Freedom; Faithfulness Guards Against the Religious Spirit

Hurrah! We are now overcoming insecurity. As we have begun to express our *real selves* in our interactions with others, we can celebrate new freedom.

Moving Forward Without Fear

In your celebration, you may be tempted to thumb your nose at those who rejected you. Having experienced insecurity and having overcome it, you want to enjoy it without becoming overconfident or proud. You may like to guard your tender new confidence, but I would also encourage you to trust in your freedom rather than become defensive or protective of yourself.

One danger that arises once we discover our "voice" is to try to impress our will upon others (whether to make up for lost time or to stretch our previously cramped wings), which until now we've been loath to do. But don't overreact. To walk in triumph is to walk in the same love and courage we learned and received when we first found Jesus. Jesus called His disciples friends if they would do what He commanded.[114] And what He commands is love.[115] As we experience our

---

[114] "*You are My friends if you do whatever I command you.*" (John 15:14)

[115] "*This is My commandment, that you love one another as I have loved you.*" (John 15:12)

transformation we can rejoice; as we remember that everything comes from God we will walk in love and remain humble.

Jesus did not attempt to impose His own will upon Judas in order to protect His own life. As we have gained self-acceptance, we must also remember to accept others unconditionally as we practice what Jesus commanded and modeled.

Until now our motive to find security has been for our survival. After years of lack, it may be tempting to retaliate and insist that others take us as we are. But this is still a cry for human acceptance. An attitude of defiance or bitterness is best resisted. Instead, let's forgive those who have wrongfully judged us, those whom we previously feared or surrendered our power to. Let us instead demonstrate the same respect toward others that we've learned to hold for ourselves, and trust our deepening self-confidence. I call this process "letting go" because it *lets go* our fears and worries, *lets go* our urge to prove we are acceptable and *lets go* of others, freeing them to make their choices. It can be scary. It can be lonely. But it is rewarding, and as we allow God's sovereignty rather than our own intention to steer our relationships, we experience deep inner peace.

Maintaining Security Without Cost to Others

Our habit in the past has been to relate from a place of fear. Now that we've found our own voice, let's grow in our awareness of others so we don't over-compensate for past times. Human nature often acts like a pendulum, swinging from one extreme to another. Let's not exchange our sense of powerlessness for a desire to dominate others. This would be expressing a *new form of our fear.*

Now that we feel confident, we may be tempted to use this confidence to make others see things or do things our way. But instead, let's surrender this temptation to God. His power is greater than any fear or temptation.[116] However unlikely it may seem, we need to be aware of this danger, and then through prayer and a study of the Word we will walk the wiser path. By meditating on powerful Scripture we can rise above temptation, bitterness and vengeful thoughts. For example, the Lord's Prayer will strengthen us.

"Our Father in heaven, Hallowed be Your name. Your kingdom come. Your will be done On earth as it is in heaven. Give us this day our daily bread. And forgive us our debts, As we forgive our debtors. And do not lead us into temptation, But deliver us from the evil one. For Yours is the kingdom and the power and the glory forever. Amen."[117]

Other Scriptures that may be particularly helpful include,

Be transformed by the renewing of your mind.[118]
An intelligent mind acquires knowledge, and the ear of the wise seeks knowledge.[119]
But grow in the grace and knowledge of our Lord and Savior Jesus Christ.[120]

As we grow in the knowledge of God, our minds will be better fortified against old temptations based on fear and ignorance. To focus on Scripture can change our thinking; at the very least it will distract us from negative thoughts.

---

[116] *There is no fear in love; but perfect love casts out fear, because fear involves torment. But he who fears has not been made perfect in love* (1 John 4:18).

[117] Matthew 6:9-13.

[118] Romans 12:2.

[119] Proverbs 18:15, RSV.

[120] 2 Peter 3:18.

*"Finally, brethren, whatever things are true, whatever things **are** noble, whatever things **are** just, whatever things **are** pure, whatever things **are** lovely, whatever things **are** of good report, if **there is** any virtue and if **there is** anything praiseworthy— meditate on these things."*[121]

As you take time to reflect on these passages, you will not only begin to better understand wisdom and foolishness, but you will also experience a transformation of the mind and gain godly wisdom.

"Study to shew thyself approved unto God, a workman that needeth not to be ashamed, rightly dividing the word of truth."[122] It is critically important that we guard our minds, because there is a force that will seek to control us by attacking and influencing our thoughts.

Super-Spiritual Dilemmas

Jesus came that we might have life and have it more abundantly.[123] Our faith in Him brings with it both freedom and responsibility. We have talked much about freedom, learning to be unhampered by fear. One of our responsibilities is to offer "life" to others, and encouragement is one way to do that. This is what is intended for all brothers and sisters in Christ. But unfortunately, as you begin to act from a place of freedom, you may encounter criticism, especially from inside the church, even though you seek to encourage. Don't be disheartened, but see this as an opportunity to grow in patience, courage and grace.

Sometimes there is confusion between responsibility and control. Control—to constrain behaviour based on misconceptions and

---

[121] Philippians 4:8.

[122] 2 Timothy 2:15, KJV.

[123] *"The thief does not come except to steal, and to kill, and to destroy. I have come that they may have life, and that they may have **it** more abundantly"* (John 10:10).

misrepresentations of God—can creep into churches or contaminate a life of faith. When religion replaces faith, freedom will get buried beneath the demands of a controlling religious spirit. Paul spoke of this throughout his letter to the Galatians. When rules replace relationship, we sacrifice God-given freedom to man-made control. I warn you most emphatically: don't do it to yourself, don't do it to others, and don't let others do it to you!

Religious Spirit Identified

"My people are destroyed for lack of knowledge."[124] There is an invisible enemy to our freedom called the *religious spirit*. While faith offers freedom, religion brings control. We need to be aware of an unseen enemy that seeks to destroy freedom through condemnation, control, oppression or manipulation. If we are ignorant, we are not equipped for combat. So let's expose the *religious spirit* and identify its motive and strategy.

Its desire is to inhibit and oppress in order to crush freedom. By exerting control upon our thinking, it seeks to destroy spontaneity, individuality and uniqueness. Before discussing more about the religious spirit, let's first compare faith with religion.

Religion is a construct of rules and regulations. It is manmade. The practice of religion is man's attempt to reach God by following this set of rules and regulations. Many religions have been invented as a means to approach God.

But religion is the opposite of faith. Faith is a gift from God, which we may receive freely. God gives us faith and is gracious to accept our repentance and faith in Jesus as enough. Through faith we have a relationship with Him; God says we are acceptable only

---

124 *"My people are destroyed for lack of knowledge. Because you have rejected knowledge, I also will reject you from being priest for Me; Because you have forgotten the law of your God, I also will forget your children"* (Hosea 4:6).

by faith.[125] Jesus came to fulfil the law and rid us of religion, yet man clings to it, because we find security in our own achievements.

Even in some contemporary thriving Christian churches, believers still operate under the assumption that we must please God through our actions; brothers and sisters in Christ still judge and impose their cultural religion on one another in the name of Christianity. Religion exists on the principle that when rules are followed, acceptability is achieved. The peculiar thing is that in religion, it is not God's benchmark that determines what is acceptable but man's. Man has put himself in the place of God as the judge. The world has given God a lot of flak for mankind's constructs. The church has given members a lot of flak in the name of Christian religiosity.

This same spirit that operates in religion also operates in secular society. The *religious spirit* is a dominating spirit and tries to dictate and control people's thoughts, actions and choices through intimidation, deceit, false guilt and oppression. We see it operate today in the "political correctness" that is imposed upon our culture. Tolerance is defined and imposed, and Christianity is sidelined because a political agenda accuses it of intolerance. We see it active in the media and in journalistic bias, where people are told what is cool and desirable, what to think and how to think.

Under the dictates of the religious spirit, failure to meet the prescribed expectations or behaviour outside the accepted decorum leads to condemnation. When we condemn ourselves for stepping out of bounds or when we feel pressure to conform, it is the religious spirit operating. Imposed expectations have nothing to do with God the Creator. He came to set us free!

---

[125] *For what does the Scripture say? "Abraham believed God, and it was accounted to him for righteousness"* (Romans 4:3).

The religious spirit is not physical, but nevertheless it is a powerful, very real influence that seeks to codify behaviour and to assert what is and is not acceptable based on a predetermined set of rules and regulations. Its mission is to assert its own way and to destroy freedom. In freedom there is life; the religious spirit hates life because it hates what departs from itself. For example, it operates in dysfunctional families who want children to conform to an image that matches the family identity rather than to celebrate each child's uniqueness. It operates in dysfunctional church families who expect everyone to have matching theology and matching behaviour. It operates in oppressive societies that outlaw freedom of thought.

As a reaction to the strict Victorian morality still influencing Western society after World War II, the sixties brought with it a sexual revolution. However, the same militant forces that imposed judgment on children born out of wedlock half a century ago now impose judgment on anti-abortionists. The religious spirit does not advocate any particular stance, only a stance that is devoid of freedom and life. Rules that evolve from morality or immorality and judgment that comes from legalistic dictates are the work of the religious spirit. A religious spirit is distinguishable not by ideology but by a stifling of freedom and a perverse determination *to have its way.*

The religious spirit is oppressive and contrary to a life of faith and freedom. It is a spirit whose motive is to combat the life-giving Spirit at the centre of our relationship with God and seeks to rob us of joy, delight and childlike expression. It seeks to control, oppress, dominate our thinking and crush our spirits with negative thoughts: condemnation and criticism. It hates what it cannot control, is bitterly opposed to free expression and detests love and peace. It is satisfied when it has its own way and is driven to crush that which opposes its will. As love is patient, kind and humble, not easily irritated, polite, forgiving, compromising, persevering, trusting, hopeful and enduring,[126] the religious spirit is its opposite: envious, self-seeking, arrogant, proud, boastful, rude, insistent, resentful, conditional and limited, taking delight in wrongdoing.

The religious spirit can influence any of us because it *provokes us* by imposing negative thoughts. C. S. Lewis personified it through the character of Wormwood in his *Screwtape Letters*.[127] In the book, Wormwood infects Patient's mind, putting into his mind proud and critical thoughts that Patient believes are his own. Lewis captured quite well the operation of the spirit that tries to impose its impression on the unsuspecting Christian. In much the same way, a religious spirit strives to manipulate our thoughts in order to create inhibition within us or conflict amongst us. The religious spirit thrives on disturbing peace and harmony. It is evil, it is ungodly; in fact it is the antagonist to relationship with God (so it is ironic and tragic that so many people believe following Jesus is a religious act).

To be ignorant of the religious spirit is dangerous to us in two ways: it seeks to infiltrate our thinking, persuading us that we need to control others to preserve our freedom, or it uses criticism—either self-imposed or from others—to oppress us personally. Awareness and the wisdom of the Holy Spirit are the keys to overcoming pressure imposed by the religious spirit.

We have just found release from insecure thoughts, so this spirit of oppression is not something we want to give any attention to. Set free from fear and self-doubt, how could we be affected by something so obviously contrary to our new joy and freedom?

---

[126] *Love suffers long **and is** kind; love does not envy; love does not parade itself, is not puffed up; does not behave rudely, does not seek its own, is not provoked, thinks no evil; does not rejoice in iniquity, but rejoices in the truth; bears all things, believes all things, hopes all things, endures all things* (1 Corinthians 13:4-7).

[127] C.S. Lewis, *The Screwtape Letters* (San Francisco: Harper, 1942).

What notions does a religious spirit use to get a grip in our heads?

Blaming Others for the Past

If we reflect on our past we will undoubtedly discover that the religious spirit has had some influence in our lives. We may well have experienced others who have tried to dominate or oppress us. It's important to recognize an issue in order to overcome or to heal from its impact, but this is not licence to lay blame or to seek revenge on others. Resist bitterness and any temptation to retaliate; in essence you would only be doing what has already been done to you. Revenge won't change the past, though if given opportunity it will block your rising above and beyond past constraints.

Now that you have recognized your insecurities and are overcoming them, it is vital that you not trap yourself by either succumbing to a temptation to blame or by becoming controlling. Even though it may be human nature to attack others as a means of self-preservation, it's important to choose to resist temptation and trust God to be your protector. Bitterness will give room to all kinds of negative attitude and behaviour. Don't start!

Rather, celebrate your liberty. Be wary of the temptation to control others and instead keep a sweet spirit of joy, hope and love. One practical strategy to overcoming is to always go to God when you want to rant or lament to someone. Going to God *first* is one of the best pieces of advice I was ever given and has kept me from developing a hardness of heart.

Judging Others

At its core, the religious spirit does not accept personal choice but rather works hard to impose its will. It plants ideas in our minds that give us an attitude that our perspective is "right" and any other is "wrong." It is what gives genuine followers of Jesus a bad reputation. How many people have rejected the notion of

Christianity, not because of what it attests but because of the imposition that some of the Christians have represented? Think of the Christian who says that dancing is wrong or rock and roll is wrong and rejects others who engage in such activities. We fall into that trap when we make assumptions of right and wrong based on a misunderstanding of the Bible.

During the 1950s and '60s many amazing and talented young people left the church because the style of their worship was seen as ungodly. Jerry Lee Lewis was one high profile example. Even Elvis Presley, who had his roots in faith, found it impossible to have his rock 'n roll accepted by the traditional church community of his time. Pop is a common style of worship music now when only a few decades ago it was considered sacrilege.

There are biblical absolutes. I am not referring to whether something such as murder is right or wrong. Rather, in this context I refer to the expressed opinion, attitude or perception that says "you must be this way" or "you must do it that way" to be a good Christian. Under the influence of the religious spirit one's attitude is self-righteous, and others must "kowtow" or they are condemned. This is not what Jesus demonstrated. He knew right from wrong. He forgave repentant sinners, He encouraged joy and freedom of expression, yet He respected law and order.

A key to recognizing the religious spirit in operation is *the way* in which a person under its influence shows objection. Righteous anger seeks to correct, not condemn. The anger of a controller is bitter, resentful and judgmental and often explodes out of control. Witness Jezebel, who would not take "no" for an answer (see 1 Kings 21:5-16) and who intimidated Elijah with threatening words that terrified the mighty prophet and caused him to flee. In the end, God destroyed her as a result of her determination to have her own way (2 Kings 9:30-37).

Religion Versus Life

In any society there are laws and rules created in an effort to keep us civilized and able to live safely and in harmony together. Laws need to be upheld. Jesus said, *"Render therefore to Caesar the things that are Caesar's, and to God the things that are God's."*[128]

But if we impose our *will*—by pressure, threat or accusation—to inhibit another man's freedom, we are exercising a religious spirit. And if in our "righteousness" we are indignant, we are most likely under the influence of the religious spirit. Legitimate certainty comes from doctrine, not opinion, and the Spirit of God convicts, whereas man's judgment condemns.

The greatest compliment we can pay a friend is in respecting his choices and his freedom to make them. If the choices are ungodly and self-destructive, we pray for the friend and exhort him, pointing him through love to God's Way. Jesus said, *"For whoever does the will of My Father in heaven is My brother and sister and mother."*[129] He accepts the choices we make—the best choice being to obey God. Our choices may not be in obedience to Him, and if not, we face consequences. However, God does not force His will on us; nor does He encourage us to impose our will upon others.

Summary

A friendship based on mutual respect is lasting. Being a friend means respecting, letting go and allowing others room to think and decide for themselves.

Using our will and imposing it upon others is ungodly.

---

[128] Matthew 22:21.

[129] Matthew 12:50.

Scriptures

> *Draw near to God and He will draw near to you* (James 4:8).

> *A friend loves at all times* (Proverbs 17:17).

> *So are the paths of all that forget God; and the hypocrite's hope shall perish* (Job 8:13, KJV).

Chapter 10

Faith, Religion or Holy Spirit: Which Gives Life?

The Religious Spirit in History

Sadly, throughout the ages the religious spirit (which is devoid of compassion) has played its part in declaring absolutes that are, in truth, only opinions. This has happened both inside and outside the Christian Church. The Crusades of the medieval period were in part a bloodbath of execution of those unbelievers who would not convert to Christianity. Later, Thomas Cromwell and the Puritan movement closed the theatres in England in an effort to curb promiscuity and to encourage piety. It was for good intentions, perhaps, that these leaders insisted that theatre in London in the 17th century be banned so that no one would be tempted by it. But forcing the ban removed personal responsibility. By removing the opportunity for individuals to decide whether theatre was "good" or "evil" for them, it stripped society and individuals of the opportunity for spiritual conviction or revelation and encouraged rebellion instead.

Trying to do the work of the Holy Spirit does not work. There is no place for the religious spirit in God's church. By contrast, during the Welsh revival of early 1900s, the Holy Spirit convicted entire towns to godliness, causing pubs and jails to sit empty as people voluntarily sought goodness and morality.

The religious spirit exists in the world and operates through people to control others. The American Prohibition of the 1920s is an example in history of a minority with strong opinion forcing a change in law. The result of revoking the relative freedom to drink alcohol was rebellion—speakeasies, liquor smuggling—as the will of a few was imposed upon the rest of that society. Similarly today in Western democracies, a loud minority seems to be dictating changes in law surrounding issues of abortion and homosexuality, changes that the majority actually disagree with.

Church Religion Is Not the Same As Faith

When man chooses *"whatever things are true…whatever things are pure"* (Philippians 4:8), it is a lovely thing. The Holy Spirit seeks to inspire our surrender to God. But this surrender is done in faith, as an act of choice. Contrarily, a religious spirit seeks to impose one man's will over another's. God sees this as controlling, oppressing the freedom Jesus died to give. He does not advocate this but instead works on a *volunteer basis.*

Jewish and church histories are full of rules that were not set by God but imposed and proclaimed as though they were doctrine. Issues over attire in church, structure of a service and raising of hands or not raising of hands are only a few of many modern examples in the church. There are serious matters regarding doctrine that are not to be compromised—the oneness of God, the divinity of Jesus, the virgin birth, for example—but relatively minor issues by comparison have split congregations and caused disillusionment and confusion in the name of religion. Christian "religion" may be man's way of attempting to get closer to godliness; however, when it ends up imposing its own will, it has failed. It may create a display of godliness on the outside as one bows to the pressure of conformity, but inside there is a crushed, stifled or even rebellious spirit.

Religious Spirit Versus Holy Spirit

The religious spirit is the enemy of God because it works to take the place of the Holy Spirit. The Holy Spirit seeks to prompt us, to convict our hearts to make more godly choices, while the religious spirit condemns or manipulates our conscience. The religious spirit attacks our will, accusing, threatening or cajoling us to do what it demands, sometimes with the motive to promote an impression of holiness.[130] The Holy Spirit, on the other hand, touches our hearts to raise our awareness and, in so doing, encourages us to make life-giving choices because we want to do so. The religious spirit says, "You must do it this way"; the Holy Spirit prompts us to consider, "What is true?" The religious spirit fears difference and opposition; the Holy Spirit has no fear, only love.

Cultural Godliness

Culture influences the way we worship God. But when culture imposes itself on our worship and is mistaken as a part of God-ordained order, then the religious spirit may be at work. Witness missionary outreach in previous centuries when around the world new disciples were told to dress, eat and behave in the same manner as the Western missionaries. It may well have been an innocent assumption to box Jesus into culture, but thank goodness we are more globally aware now and seek to touch lives and hearts through the gospel alone. Praise God that numerous missionary societies have learned from past mistakes and do this very thing!

---

[130] "*...the scribes and the Pharisees sit in Moses' seat. Therefore whatever they tell you to observe, **that** observe and do, but do not do according to their works; for they say, and do not do*" (Matthew 23:2-3).

Security: Found in Religion or in Relationship?

Religion is the practice of rules or regulations in an attempt to draw toward God. To practice religion, we conform to manmade rules we believe make us right with God. It is a bit like a list where, if we accomplish all the items God is pleased or appeased, and we can rest confident in ourselves. Out of this security can grow self-satisfaction, which leads to self-righteousness. (It certainly leads to self-sufficiency, where we don't need a relationship with God because we just do what we are supposed to do, according to our religion, to satisfy Him.) What exists outside our religion is condemned. This attitude is a breeding ground for a religious spirit—right behaviour is acceptable, wrong behaviour is unacceptable, and we are in charge of the gavel to decide. The practice of religion offers a false sense of security based on our works—abilities, achievements and following the rules laid down for us.

On the other hand, faith leaves us more vulnerable. Inherent in faith is relationship, and relationship as practiced in the Christian faith is based on a relationship with the God of the universe, who reaches out to us and offers unconditional love. Relationship is scary and makes us vulnerable, but only through our vulnerability can we *genuinely* receive from God what cannot be offered through religion.

By its very nature relationship is dynamic. When we risk and express freely who we are, we discover that we are accepted, and we experience such an absolute sense of liberty, joy and love that we move far beyond the false security we experience if we remain inside religion's box.

Details about the religious spirit may seem to be a digression from the topic of emotional security; however, understanding the religious spirit is, I believe, imperative to protect our freedom and our fragile confidence. Such awareness will help guard us from fear and prejudice and from the need to control and help us to walk in an attitude of respect toward others.

A Personal Experience: the Religious Spirit As Bully

The religious spirit works through young and old. I mentioned that when I was a little girl another girl bullied me in school. She was my age and in my class. We'll call her Nancy. Nancy impressed upon others that they should not be my friend. I was taunted throughout the school day by Nancy and others, who agreed either vocally or by taking their place next to Nancy.

For whatever reason, Nancy needed to target someone to pick on, and I was that person. She must have had her own grief and inner turmoil, but who can say why a child is unkind to another? I believe what she was manifesting in her behaviour at that young age of nine, ten and eleven was the religious spirit. She was wilfully seeking to control interaction between others, to decide who was acceptable, who was not and how to manage the situation. It was an incredibly painful three-year experience for me.

When it came time to move on to secondary school, Nancy told her then best friend that if she didn't choose the same school as Nancy, Nancy would no longer be her friend. Clearly, Nancy had a propensity to dominate. Fortunately for Nancy's best friend, she had the courage to opt for a different school.

It is good news that in adulthood Nancy expressed regret for her bullying behaviour, and good news too that I had no need for an apology; I had not harboured any judgment upon her. In fact I was blessed by that experience because through it I learned compassion.

Worship in Church

There has been much issue made in some denominations about the area of worship in the church. Shall we dance? Shall we raise our hands? Shall we kneel in prayer? Which one is the "right" way to worship? When King David danced wearing a scant covering, his wife Mical mocked him (2 Samuel 6:12–23). Yet it was she who bore humiliation as she had no children. This book is not to discuss styles of worship, but it is important to note that God welcomes worship and does not define style. He does say that things should be done in order.[131] When backbiting, criticism and imposition move in a church, covertly or overtly, there is a stifling of the freedom Jesus came to release. David danced—and he was a man after God's own heart.[132] As we worship Him in spirit and in truth,[133] the specifics of how we worship surely are left to individuals and are not doctrine or rule.

Submission and Respect of Authority

Equally important to our freedom of expression is our responsibility to submit to authority, for that is God's order. If an individual experiences intimidation from a church leader, that leader may well be under the influence of a religious spirit. Confronting directly and peaceably, pressing through and forgiving are the steps I suggest. Obedience to our spiritual leaders is godly; there is no place for rebellion in Christlike humility. But while acting in obedience, with grace and directness, one has the freedom to express disagreement and seek

---

[131] *but all things should be done decently and in order* (1 Corinthians 14:40, RSV).

[132] *"David the* **son** *of Jesse,* **a man after My own heart**, *who will do all My will"* (Act 13:22).

[133] *"God is Spirit, and those who worship Him must worship in spirit and truth"* (John 4:24).

to resolve differences. In private, we work to forgive the intimidation or close-mindedness of the leader. Remember, we do not oppose our leaders but battle unseen forces that attack both of us.[134] If we choose to rebel we are only blocking relationship, which God so wants His people to share. Instead, by being obedient we encourage the one in authority to soften his stance. Through gentle yet confident directness, we lift ourselves above the oppression of the religious spirit, and we keep open the possibility of renewed and deeper relationship.

Am I Religious?

Knowing our motives enhances our relationships. Do we recognize our own motives? If not, let's develop that awareness. Why we do something is as important as what we do. Apology and making amends are important responsibilities when the aim is to strengthen communication and to build bridges. But if we are seeking to appease someone or our aim is to avoid rejection, then our motive is self-seeking and our actions will not build up the other person or improve our relationship with them.[135]

---

134 *For we do not wrestle against flesh and blood, but against principalities, against powers, against the rulers of the darkness of this age, against spiritual **hosts** of wickedness in the heavenly **places*** (Ephesians 6:12)

135 *That we should no longer be children, tossed to and fro and carried about with every wind of doctrine, by the trickery of men, in the cunning craftiness of deceitful plotting, but, speaking the truth in love, may grow up in all things into Him who is the head—Christ—from whom the whole body, joined and knit together by what every joint supplies, according to the effective working by which every part does its share, causes growth of the body for the edifying of itself in love. This I say, therefore, and testify in the Lord, that you should no longer walk as the rest of the Gentiles walk, in the futility of their mind, having their understanding darkened, being alienated from the life of God, because of the ignorance that is in them, because of the blindness of their heart; who, being past feeling, have given themselves over to lewdness, to work all uncleanness with greediness* (Ephesians 4:14-19).

A motive at the other extreme is to prove we are right. This does nothing to build relationship but instead creates walls between people. If we seek to develop our sensitivity to others' vulnerability, we learn to exercise compassion and kindness. As we focus on building the self-esteem of others, ours will also rise. It is good to focus on giving, and better than arguing!

As a teenager I had a poster that said "If you love something, set it free; if it comes back, it is yours; if it doesn't, it never was." It is sentimental and untrue, but there is something of value in it. It is essential, I believe, to allow others freedom to consider and to decide their own point of view, just as we are free to do likewise. What we sow we will reap. By giving our respect to others we sow into them a sense of personal responsibility; as we grow, God will entrust us with greater and deeper responsibility.

Seventeenth century British theatres eventually reopened to great joy and celebration; American prohibition ended (although a type of organized crime that ascended during that time still plagues American society today). Any relationship that is free will grow; any that is controlled will die. Even God gives us the freedom to obey or disobey Him. He simply promises never to give up on us while still having His own identity, not dependant upon ours. So let's take a small risk in our relationships by giving the same life-giving freedom to others that we have most graciously been offered and have received.

Strength in Surrendering

Emotional strength comes not from strengthening our will but from surrendering it to the Holy Spirit. Jesus, before the trial and the cross, said, "*Father, if it Your will, take this cup away from Me; nevertheless not My will, but Yours, be done.*"[136] How did He

---

[136] Luke 22:42.

get to that place? Through prayer. Likewise, we can declare our surrender.

To begin the process of surrender, I learned to tell the Lord in prayer that "I submit my body to my soul (will, emotion, mind), my soul to my spirit, and my spirit to the Holy Spirit." There is power in speaking out, giving over to God purposefully and deliberately. It releases and enables us to be fully submitted to the power and presence of the Holy Spirit. He will not override our will; instead, as we surrender to Him, we give Him authority to intervene, which enables us to overcome our undesirable habits. It certainly is only through His power that we can overcome.

Just as only God can save, only God in us can overcome the old with the new. *"For God did not give us a spirit of timidity but a spirit of power and love and self-control."*[137] Abraham was called a friend of God because of his faith.[138] When we put our faith in God alone, we receive His friendship. As His friends we receive through faith all He has—His peace, His love and His emotional stability.

Marriage: Trusting the Security Bond

A savings bond is something that is paid for and held to be redeemed at a later date, at which time it will have increased in value. To have a savings bond is a guaranteed asset; likewise is a bond of marriage.

"Therefore a man shall leave his father and mother and be joined to his wife, and they shall become one flesh."[139] When we are tied together

---

[137] *"For God has not given us a spirit of fear, but of power and of love and of a sound mind"* (2 Timothy 1:7, RSV. NKJV).

[138] *And the Scripture was fulfilled which says, "Abraham believed God, and it was accounted to him for righteousness." And he was called the friend of God* (James 2:23).

[139] Genesis 2:24.

in marriage we give and receive of ourselves and we learn from one another. Our bond or union as partners makes us stronger. In marriage, the security of the promise to stay together gives us the freedom to be ourselves. Sometimes we may take this for granted and push the limit of our spouse's patience! Yet, we can trust the love is guaranteed, or *unconditional*. In a good marriage we may agree to disagree.

God calls His people, the church, His "*bride*" (Revelation 21:9). He wants us to trust that bond and be trustworthy too. As we cleave to Him, our "marriage relationship" with Him and the body of believers makes us stronger and more secure, which affects all our human relationships. When our anchor is in Christ, we can be confident that neither fear nor intimidation nor oppression can threaten us. The religious spirit that seeks its security through conformity cannot affect us, because instead we dwell in intimacy with God. Ideally the entire church family interacts with this love, and our relationships nurture mutual growth, spiritual development and fulfilment. If all believers lived out this knowledge and spiritual power, such would be the case. So let us not doubt or hold back. That our spirits are reborn, saved by grace through faith is true, but let us also receive the knowledge and walk in the truth that we are reborn emotionally too. He has not saved us in part, but in full. That, "*neither death nor life, nor angels nor principalities nor powers, nor things present nor things to come, nor height nor depth, nor any other created thing, shall be able to separate us from the love of God which is in Christ Jesus our Lord.*"[140]

Giving Our Love

Perfect love casts out all fear. When we love we willingly surrender our will, secure in the knowledge that we will be loved in return.

---

[140] Romans 8:38-39.

William Sydney Porter (O. Henry) was an American storyteller who wrote a love story, *The Gift of the Magi,* about a poor young couple. At Christmas, each wanted to give the other a gift to show their commitment and love. The wife had magnificent long beautiful hair. She cut it and sold it in order to buy her husband a fob chain for his inherited pocket watch; the husband adored his wife's hair so he sold his only prized possession, his watch, and bought hair combs for his wife. The story is a bittersweet one. Each, loving the other, sacrificed all he or she had to give generously to the other. God's love is like that. When we recognize and trust His love, we can give to others, secure in the knowledge that His love will never leave or forsake us.

Summary

> Wisest choices are made from the knowledge of God through the Holy Spirit.
>
> The Holy Spirit, not our strength of will, empowers us to overcome our fears.
>
> Our relationship with God has the intimacy of a marriage bond, and we can live in the assurance that He is more than able to provide.

Scriptures

> *For He Himself has said, "I will never leave you nor forsake you"* (Hebrews 13:5b).

> *For I am not ashamed of the gospel of Christ, for it is the power of God to salvation for everyone who believes* (Romans 1:16).

Chapter 11

Love in All Circumstances

"Judge not, that you be not judged."[141] As we love, so we will receive, because such is the principle of sowing and reaping. What you give you will receive, so if you give love, you will receive...perhaps not from the source you expect, but you will receive. We love because we are commanded to and because it is beneficial to others. Through that expression of love, we will, in turn, have our needs fulfilled. Reading on from this verse, we see that Jesus said, *"for with the judgment you pronounce you will be judged"* (Matthew 7:2, RSV).

Do unto Others

Love accepts. Love is the opposite of judgment. While it is not blind to weaknesses or shortcomings, it doesn't seek to criticize, change or reject others. By its very nature, agape focuses on giving rather than receiving love. The power of this love comes from God. To release it without the help of the Holy Spirit will be exhaustive and draining. But with the Holy Spirit to support and to teach and to guide us, and with discernment to know when to give and when to let go, we learn to sow love into the church and into society. Agape goes beyond fear and rejection

---

[141] Matthew 7:1.

because it requires nothing. Agape is perfect love. *"Perfect love casts out fear."*[142]

Perfect Love

Godly love conquers all.

Eros love is that of sexuality and romance. Philio love is brotherly love. Agape is the unconditional love we receive from God. As we learn to give away the love He gives to us, we empower others as He empowers us. Jesus died and rose to save us, and so He conquered death. Through Jesus, agape conquers all.

Perfect Love Is Possible, but Not in Our Own Strength

We know it is vital to our security to rise above thoughts and feelings that produce emotional insecurity and that perfect love holds the key to our security. So how do we to achieve this "perfect" solution? How can we strive to attain perfect love?

First, be encouraged: it is possible to love perfectly. Jesus said, *"Therefore you shall be perfect, just as your Father in heaven is perfect."*[143] In His eyes, to be perfect in love, as part of our perfection, is achievable. *"With men this is impossible, but with God all things are possible."*[144]

The Practice of Agape

Matthew chapter 7 is the last of three chapters recording Jesus' famous Sermon on the Mount. There, He addressed the lack of love in us and the issue of judgment: *"And why do you look at the speck in your brother's eye, but do not consider the plank in your own eye?"*[145]

---

[142] 1 John 4:18.

[143] Matthew 5:48.

[144] Matthew 19:26.

[145] Matthew 7:3.

The first practical step in the approach to growing more accepting and loving of others is to overcome every tendency to condemn others. Having a tendency to be too hard on oneself is an important though opposite threat, which I'll address in part V. By considering our own faults and bringing to remembrance our own shortcomings, we can keep a healthy perspective concerning the frailties and failings of others. I have found my opinions to be completely detrimental to relationship, and they have hindered my ability to love. Whenever I *expect* something from others based on my cultural opinions of what is good or bad behaviour, I become disillusioned or critical.

Instead, when I look for the positive in others and ignore nagging or petty thoughts that rise up when I want or expect something, I keep a sweet spirit and a sweet attitude toward my fellow man. Years ago, my husband was asked to take pictures at the wedding of an acquaintance. He was invited to the wedding. Feeling insecure in my relationships, I was hurt and felt strongly I should be invited as well. I grew bitter at being left out. It took time for me to realize that my expectation was based on opinion and insecurity. I learned, as the bride was gracious to me, that the occasion was more important than my expectation or hurt feelings. I experienced grace and learned that my opinionated nature was a barrier to relationship.

Motive

"*Or how can you say to your brother, 'Let me remove the speck from your eye'; and look, a plank **is** in your own eye?*"[146] We may strive to try to change others in order to make life more comfortable for ourselves, but under the guise of wanting to help them. We need to be aware of not only our own shortcomings but our

---

[146] Matthew 7:4.

motives as well. It is easier to be forgiving of others and to accept them as they are when we recognize shortcomings in ourselves.

Motive lies behind action. It is the root of behaviour and attitude, the fuel we need to progress from desire to achievement. In our humanity we are driven to survive, and to be loved makes the living worthwhile. We will go to great lengths to sustain life and love. Locked inside our brains are our personal beliefs for survival, derived from our earlier experiences and relationships. Each of these rationalizations becomes a motive: some are dark—such as vengeance; others are uplifting or *light*—such as encouragement or giving joy. What they all have in common is "me-centredness." However, when the desire is the giving of love for its own sake (rather than to love in order to be loved), when the motive is purely to share Jesus' love, that motive has become "other-centred," which cannot be controlled by fear or loneliness. This is agape. As we become aware of our self-centred nature we can let it go and move with generosity and God's grace.

Agape is available, and Jesus' life models it for us to see and to receive. When we are in relationship with God and experience His forgiveness, it becomes far easier to forgive. Through our experience of forgiveness, we recognize His love and become better equipped to offer it to others.

Seeing in a Mirror

By discovering our flaws and our concealed motives, we discover our very character. Staring at our own character enables us to see our sin and shame, the hypocrisy Jesus speaks of in Matthew 7: "*Hypocrite! First remove the plank from your own eye, and then you will see clearly to remove the speck from your brother's eye.*"[147]

---

[147] Matthew 7:5.

Our choice is to deny or to repent of our flaws. If we deny, we continue to live the old way, ensnared by our criticism of others and anxiety within. But as we repent and receive forgiveness, love and rebirth pushes out what we hate in ourselves. In exchange, we receive more of what God created in us and loves. With His help we will change. Discovering the truth in us is the catalyst for setting us free.

> *"Ask, and it will be given to you; seek, and you will find; knock, and it will be opened to you. For everyone who asks receives, and he who seeks finds, and to him who knocks it will be opened. Or what man is there among you who, if his son asks for bread, will give him a stone? Or if he asks for a fish, will he give him a serpent? If you then, being evil, know how to give good gifts to your children, how much more will your Father who is in heaven give good things to those who ask Him! Therefore, whatever you want men to do to you, do also to them, for this is the Law and the Prophets."*[148]

The Miraculous Freedom of Forgiveness

Once we ask to be forgiven, it becomes increasingly easier to forgive. Life is a journey, and so we will keep making mistakes and asking forgiveness for the new mistakes we make. Along the way we learn humility and practice forgiveness. Each time we are forgiven, we feel loved, and with each trial we get better at loving. The old adage "practice makes perfect" proves true!

By learning how to love and forgive, by being empowered by God's Holy Spirit to do so, we become less and less anxious for ourselves.

---

[148] Matthew 7:7-12.

Finally, brethren, whatever things are true, whatever things ***are*** *noble, whatever things* ***are*** *just, whatever things* ***are*** *pure, whatever things* ***are*** *lovely, whatever things* ***are*** *of good report, if* ***there is*** *any virtue and if* ***there is*** *anything praiseworthy— meditate on these things. The things which you learned and received and heard and saw in me, these do, and the God of peace will be with you.*[149]

Summary

God offers agape love, the unconditional love we all crave. By receiving this kind of love we gain a sense of emotional security.

A natural opportunity that results from receiving agape is learning to give it. What we sow, we shall reap. Our journey to freedom then is about growing in our ability to share the agape of Jesus.

Agape is the opposite of judgment. To practice agape means to choose to relinquish our judgment of others.

Learning to forgive ourselves is an important step in the successful practice of agape.

Knowing our motives is key to discovering our character. Understanding our character sparks the opportunity for change. Choosing to accept what we discover about ourselves is fuel for the change.

Scriptures

"And you shall know the truth, and the truth shall make you free" (John 8:32).

Beloved, let us love one another, for love is of God; and everyone who loves is born of God and knows God. He who does not love

---

[149] Philippians 4: 8-9.

*does not know God, for God is love. In this the love of God was manifested toward us, that God has sent His only begotten Son into the world, that we might live through Him. In this is love, not that we loved God, but that He loved us and sent His Son to **be the** propitiation for our sins. Beloved, if God so loved us, we also ought to love one another. No one has seen God at any time. If we love one another, God abides in us, and His love has been perfected in us* (1 John 4:7-12).

Summary of Part IV

Learning to trust our own perceptions and learning simultaneously how to discern the character of others will assist us in our efforts to maintain greater security. Until now, perhaps the track record hasn't been good in our choice of relationships. But now is the time to improve that record. A relationship based on truthfulness and respect will build our own character while also demonstrating the character of our friends. Our relationships are now to be built on encouragement and the strengthening of one another.

Believers are to have their deepest relationships with those who also share knowledge of Father, Jesus and the Holy Spirit; otherwise the most important dimension of their character and person will go unfed.

We need to trust God and ourselves and let go! Freedom in our relationships opposes the religious spirit and is the difference between our giving assurance and being a bully.

Finally, love has the power to heal all fear, brokenness and insecurity.

Staying Free
Maintaining Security,
Growing in Character

Chapter 12

Developing the Character of Christ: From Pride through Forgiveness to Humility

It's all very well to discover how we became insecure and to learn to overcome it. But unless we are transformed from within, we will continue to battle our old ways of thinking and exhaust ourselves. The way to maintain our security is to keep growing forward. The way to grow forward is to live a life as full of the Spirit (and devoid of the flesh) as possible.

"Not my will but Yours" sets us free from an agenda that would rob us of peace. Surrender and trust enable us to follow God's will. Prayer and praise strengthen and guide us to know His will and the way we should go. When my attention is off me I am less likely to get caught up in former destructive thinking patterns; when attention is on God I am encouraged and refreshed, able to see more clearly a healthy perspective or the next step to take.

Embracing Challenge

It starts with having the attitude that difficult situations are opportunities to help me grow. Challenges and hurdles are a part of life. One who walks secure in the Lord receives those challenges and hurdles as gifts, knowing that the most trying times give us the best opportunities for growth. As we engage with life we will face challenges that will test our sense of identity and security. As our confidence and faith grow, how we respond to challenges will be transformed. We will see evidence of this in the grace we both demonstrate and receive.

I can't say how often that, following prayer and surrender, I have realized I handled a situation with the patience or wisdom I had prayed for. Difficult situations give us the opportunity to discover how we have changed. Just as lifting weights makes us stronger physically, facing interpersonal situations that seem to threaten our safety reveals to us how much we have overcome our fears. Challenge is the means by which we can discover our mettle!

Developing a Realistic Self-Image: How Loss Brought Self-Revelation

Challenges lead us to self-discovery. As I discover more about me, I can surrender to the Lord the aspects about me that are ungodly. When I consider Scripture, I can apply it to my life to evaluate my progress. For example, Jesus said, *"Judge not, that you be not judged."*[150] There was a particular moment in my life when I applied that text to a situation, and I overcame a bad habit overnight.

For as long as I can remember, I had difficulty forgiving myself. I was a high achiever. High expectations and the ability to produce made me prideful. I punished myself for failure and was very unforgiving of my mistakes. Then, in the turn of one day, I learned to forgive myself.

Learning to forgive myself means allowing God to judge me instead of me judging myself. He has said "Do not judge," which includes the cycle of subjective self-flagellation we exercise when we think we haven't done nearly as well as we thought we were capable of. Allow me to explain by example.

---

[150] Matthew 7:1.

One afternoon, while sitting on my living room carpet, I was mentally beating myself up for making a bad decision. It was habit for me to berate myself for days, or weeks, or even months whenever I perceived I had made a mistake. What triggered this occasion was a decision I'd made to decline a job offer. I came to realize too late that I had turned away a blessing and missed a golden opportunity. So, upon recognizing my "mistake," I began my usual lengthy emotional spiral into self-criticism and self-doubt, with an added touch of self-pity.

These interludes of self-torture will be familiar to anyone who tends to expect perfection. In hindsight I see that it was a sign of pride. I was surprised by my failure because I was over-confident about making decisions. I fell short of my aspirations because I tried to prove myself and left God out of the equation. Now by punishing myself for the decision I was still leaving God out of the picture.

When I first realized my mistake I was devastated. I felt shame, regret and sorrow; I had worked hard, only to miss an opportunity that had sprung from my effort and my prayer. There is everything right with diligence, hard work and optimism. However, my motive had been purely self-centred. I suggest that to wrap our identity in achievement and to hope for success to the extent that our self-image and emotions hang on the result are prideful. (It is also an example of acceptance-by-doing rather than of grace-by-being.)

To know and to accept who we are, exclusive of result, is a new aim. I have learned that my willing attitude and availability matters to God, but the result is much more up to Him. This has taught me to be kinder to myself, to accept myself as I am today and to surrender that "self" to the Lord for His pruning.[151] It has taken humility for me to accept my limitations, but in doing so I've also

---

151 *"Every branch in Me that does not bear fruit He takes away; and every **branch** that bears fruit He prunes, that it may bear more fruit"* (John 15:2).

become better at forgiving myself, and ironically I've become a more capable person. Learning to forgive myself has given me new freedom, which has enabled me to think more clearly and to execute with more certainty.

The Humility of Jesus

Jesus was infinitely confident and infinitely humble. He modelled confidence that came from knowing He was loved by the Father[152] and did only what His Father directed Him to do.[153] Likewise, we can be completely confident, knowing that we "*can do all things through Christ who strengthens,*"[154] and be fully humble, knowing that "*by grace you have been saved by faith, and that not of yourselves; it is the gift of God, not of works, lest anyone should boast.*"[155] We can surrender our decisions to Him and allow Him to guide us. It doesn't mean never making a decision again, but it does mean that we have our wise Father always guiding us. When the road is unclear or particularly difficult, He will help us to see the fuller picture.

Let God Be the Judge

My desire is that we learn to identify and accept our strengths and weaknesses from a realistic and balanced perspective. As we expand our openness toward God, we become more willing to learn from Him and to accept His judgment and direction, and we are emotionally healthier and more at peace with ourselves.

---

[152] *And suddenly a voice **came** from heaven, saying, "This is My beloved Son, in whom I am well pleased"* (Matthew 3:17).

[153] *Then Jesus answered and said to them, "Most assuredly, I say to you, the Son can do nothing of Himself, but what He sees the Father do; for whatever He does, the Son also does in like manner"* (John 5:19).

[154] Philippians 4:13.

[155] Ephesians 2:8-9.

Communion with God is a better prescription for health and success than self-imposed criticism.

Self-scrutiny and self-awareness do play a part in our transformation. Sustained transformation begins in the prayer closet. For me it is literally spending time on the carpet before God. When I ask God to show me what needs pruning, He does. To begin, I may be impacted by a verse of Scripture or something I hear in a sermon. I may have an impression in my mind to explore through prayer or an emotional response to something that is far deeper than the situation warrants. Once I have a starting place, I ask the Lord to lead me. As I wait He brings to mind a memory that makes me understand where He is leading me. Tears and repentance are sure to come.

Sometimes in the process it feels intense and heavy, but frequently I have found it seems worst just before a breakthrough in my circumstances and this carries me through. When I am inevitably brought toward God, I have a good cry and then sense release and an end to the pain that has long been buried. This is the end of the journey, and I rise up, literally and figuratively, released from a memory and a flaw that had constricted me for days or years.

We already know that learning to forgive others is imperative if we are to live in freedom. Forgiveness is a valuable gift. I have learned that learning to forgive myself is equally important. Letting God be God in my life means allowing Him to show me the best way forward. Once I realized that my habit of self-condemnation was ungodly and surrendered judgment to Him, I became free from that habit. By deciding to allow God to be my judge I became more open to learning and growing in humility and grace. I felt such relief when I realized that being too hard on myself was something God actually did not want me to do!

Conviction Versus Condemnation

"And when He [the Holy Spirit] has come, He will convict the world of sin, and of righteousness, and of judgment."[156] My personal experience of Holy Spirit conviction is of the gentle, persistent still small voice that tells me I have done wrong. There is no sense of shame. The voice humbles me, draws me closer to God, and I am grateful for His love and acceptance. I thrive on His correction. Surrender sets me free from the character flaw, and exposure protects me from pride.

Alternatively, when condemnation comes, it is an accusing voice that brings with it despair, oppression and humiliation. It draws me into myself (and away from God). The voice lies to me, telling me I can fix the flaw or cover it up or blame someone else for it. To listen to this voice will bring self-destruction or hardness of heart. It feeds my pride and independence from God.

Pride is the most despised of sin. It is what caused Lucifer to be banished. An angel of heaven, he was cast down to earth because he dared to attempt to be as God (Isaiah 14:12–15). He became Satan, prowling the earth (1 Peter 5:8) *"to and fro"* (Job 2:2), with the aim of devouring people with his lies. He uses condemnation to crush the spirit of hope and life within us. The one source able to drive out pride is the Holy Spirit.

I describe this to you so that you can escape these tricks of our enemy Satan. The voice of condemnation speaks a lie or a half-truth and is soul-destroying.

---

[156] John 16:8.

The Proverbial Log in Our Eye: Looking Within to Expose Our Darker Side

Truly, the truth shall set us free.[157] I understand Jesus to be endorsing the pursuit of truth when He says, *"first take the log out of your own eye."*[158] As I examine my motives and my behaviour, my character improves, and I mature.

We tend to learn far more from our mistakes than our triumphs. But just as we need the awareness of error in order to grow, so too do we need the hope of victory to persevere. Condemnation offers no hope and no room for growth, whereas conviction from the Holy Spirit and a humble, positive attitude toward discovering our short-comings inspires us to new life.[159] Each of us is responsible for our own actions, and we must bear the consequences for our own mistakes. Looking honestly at ourselves from time to time is not the same as judgment, which brings with it condemnation.

Healthy self-esteem needs to develop from within. Our attitude and response to external criticism reveals the image we have of ourselves. If we react to criticism defensively—with rage, vindictiveness, or bitterness—we recognize that we are not healed and have adopted a heightened sense of self-esteem that we aim to protect. Conversely, a low level of self-esteem is evident when criticism results in depression, deep sorrow or hopeless regret. Both responses show little recognition of universal human frailty. If we cannot accept our limitations as something that, since the

---

[157] *"And you shall know the truth, and the truth shall make you free"* (John 8:32).

[158] Matthew 7:5, RSV.

[159] *All Scripture is given by inspiration of God, and is profitable for doctrine, for reproof, for correction, for instruction in righteousness, that the man of God may be complete, thoroughly equipped for every good work* (2 Timothy 3:16-17).

fall of man, all experience, we have not got a realistic perspective of ourselves.

Fortunately, God's objective and holistic view offers balance. The Holy Spirit convicts us but does not condemn.[160] We are made aware of our sins through the Spirit; yet God accepts us in spite of these weaknesses. Just as He asks us to learn to accept imperfections in others, He wants us to see and to accept our own and to trust that He accepts us too. While this book does not encompass every possible angle to finding freedom, examining our shortcomings sheds light into our hearts. When darkness is exposed, the light ultimately brings truth and freedom.

The final aspect to self-discovery is to address the motives behind our search. As we seek truth or a deeper relationship with the Lord or a greater understanding of ourselves and others, we will find blessing in our search. But if our motive goes beyond that, aiming to build up our self-esteem or to yield greater accomplishment or a higher profile in His service or the world, we may be striving to grow, but it is to gain a reward beyond itself. *"Love suffers long **and** is kind; love does not envy; love does not parade itself, is not puffed up."*[161] Self-scrutiny may lead to godly behaviour, but unless it is as an end in itself it is for the wrong motive.

"That which is born of the flesh is flesh, and that which is born of the Spirit is spirit."[162] If we try to do something to gain something else, we are working apart from God; we are working in our flesh. A sincere, heartfelt gesture toward others is humble and loving and builds relationship. Conversely, to display self-loathing or to make self-denigrating comments may be a defense

---

[160] ***There is*** *therefore now no condemnation to those who are in Christ Jesus, who do not walk according to the flesh, but according to the Spirit* (Romans 8:1).

[161] 1 Corinthians 13:4.

[162] John 3:6.

mechanism—an attempt to prevent someone else from criticizing first. To be transparent, expressing our pain sincerely so that relationship can be built, will bring not only healing but healthy intimacy with others as well. So, as we strive to grow, let's be aware that our motive can get clouded and complicated. *"For let not that man suppose that he will receive anything from the Lord; **he** is a double-minded man, unstable in all his ways."*[163]

View Any Experience As for Our Good

I mentioned earlier that when I was a child others bullied me. It was a horrible three years of my childhood, which affected me far into my future as well. But that experience, although painful, taught me compassion. If I had not discovered the pain of rejection then, I would not have become sensitive to it and might have hurt others through insensitivity and rejection. Ultimately, all experience is for good and will yield benefits if we allow it. Our past can teach us, and we will grow.

Joseph with the multicoloured coat said this to his brothers, who had betrayed him: *"But as for you, you meant evil against me; **but** God meant it for good, in order to bring it about as **it is** this day."*[164] Joseph spent years in slavery and prison, growing in character, before being entrusted as a ruler of Egypt and the preserver of nations during seven years of famine. His experience was his opportunity, and he embraced it to grow in maturity. As we grow in character, we discover and value ourselves and grow in security.

Growing in Humility

We have seen how recognizing our own shortcomings enables us to accept others more readily and that learning to love others

---

163 James 1:7-8.

164 Genesis 50:20.

unconditionally teaches us to love ourselves. On a final note, in facing the challenges of life with an attitude of grace, we grow in humility.

Why is humility desirable? Humility is not a show of weakness or failure. Nor is it false modesty. And it is not humble to be a target for mockery or persecution. Humility is the knowledge and acceptance of personal strength and ability without pride or the need for attention. It is the awareness that there are others more able. It responds modestly in success and with dignity in failure. Humility knows that above all else, *there but for the grace of God I go.*[165]

We may face trials that make us look bad, but if we are humble people we will not fear how others will perceive us. We know our ability and standard and do not fear others' perceptions of us; nor are we ashamed. Trial is our only teacher. Those with little need to prove have learned much about humility. Alternatively, if it is painful to admit a mistake, it signals that our pride is taking a bashing. While that may be very human, it reveals a character flaw.

Humility is pride's antithesis. It enables us to recognize our limitations without crushing our confidence. As we grow in humility—and shrink in pride—we are less shocked by our failures, less daunted by our need to change, and more willing to apologize to others, to ourselves and to God.

Jesus, the greatest teacher on earth, told His disciples that He came not to be served but to serve, and He instructed them to do likewise.[166] He washed the dusty, sandal-shorn feet of each of them to demonstrate humility in service (John 13:3–11). He is our ultimate example.

---

[165] John Bradford (1510-1555) evangelical preacher burned at the stake.

[166] *"Whoever desires to become great among you, let him be your servant. And whoever desires to be first among you, let him be your slave—just as the Son of Man did not come to be served, but to serve, and to give His life a ransom for many"* (Matthew 20:26-28).

The confident person and the humble person are one and the same. Great confidence flows out of humility, and service flows from the broad shoulders of the humble person. The humble person is not focused on himself. His confidence is in God, and his security is rock-solid.

The ultimate source from which we draw humility is the Holy Spirit. Our actions can imitate, but the power that transforms our character from pride to humility is the Holy Spirit's. Having received Jesus into our lives, we have the Holy Spirit in us. But unless we surrender our pride and seek to develop humility, the Holy Spirit will be inhibited. He can convict us by showing us where we are prideful and will transform us through supernatural revelation and natural day-to-day experiences if we give Him time and attention. He helps us to dispense with pride as we meet it, face to face, in circumstances that arise. When we avail ourselves of these opportunities to grow, we are transformed into the likeness of Christ, from one state of glory to the next.

Salvation Is for This Life As Well As the Next

God's forgiveness is available to all those who ask. But salvation is not just for eternal life beyond our mortal existence in this world. Salvation rescues us from the strife of this world too, and from inner torment. By receiving God's unconditional forgiveness through faith in Jesus, we receive the Holy Spirit and all the blessings and freedom He offers.

Paul encouraged all who live for the Lord to "*walk worthy of the calling with which you were called, with all lowliness and gentleness, with longsuffering, bearing with one another in love, endeavoring to keep the unity of the Spirit in the bond of peace.*"[167] I suggest that we extend that context to include ourselves, so that we may recognize

---

[167] Ephesians 4:1b-3.

patience, meekness and the love of God. He will enable us to be strengthened by His grace and to be transformed into patient, meek, loving, gracious individuals, secure and confident in Him and therefore in ourselves.

Forgiving myself is as important as any other step in my journey to emotional security. Asking God to convict me and submitting to Him enables God to show me where and how I need to grow. He reveals to me those areas where I am vulnerable and heals me.

Summary

Forgiveness includes forgiving myself. God has said, "Do not judge." I believe that includes not judging ourselves. A high achiever in particular can find it difficult to be forgiving of himself.

If we invite Him, God will highlight our strengths and weaknesses in a way that will encourage us to grow.

Healthy self-scrutiny will not result in condemnation. It is out of a healthy attitude to growth and change that we can remain emotionally secure when our behaviour or character is challenged.

Motive for seeking change will affect growth; be alert to the human tendency to double-mindedness.

The Holy Spirit best enables us to grow in humility. Humility rescues us from pride.

The power of the Holy Spirit is freely available to all who confess God and believe and follow Jesus as His son.

Salvation is for today as much as it is for eternity. Salvation is rescue from emotional strife as much as from physical death.

Scriptures

> *And be kind to one another, tenderhearted, forgiving one another, even as God in Christ forgave you* (Ephesians 4:32).

> *Therefore, as **the** elect of God, holy and beloved, put on tender mercies, kindness, humility, meekness, longsuffering; bearing with one another, and forgiving one another, if anyone has a complaint against another; even as Christ forgave you, so you also **must** do* (Colossians 3:12-13).

> *And the LORD passed before him and proclaimed, "The LORD, the LORD God, merciful and gracious, longsuffering, and abounding in goodness and truth, keeping mercy for thousands, forgiving iniquity and transgression and sin"* (Exodus 34:6-7).

Chapter 13

Rejecting Doubt, Embracing the L-Curve: Personal Maturity and Maturity Within the Church

We have overcome our fears and feel secure in ourselves. Now we are hungry to grow and even have a prayer mechanism to help us. In ourselves we are growing in confidence. How can we be sure to translate what we've acquired personally into our relationships?

We need to remain teachable in order to grow, and many messages will lead us toward maturity. But some will not. We cannot use pain as a litmus test, because growth almost necessarily includes pain (hence the cliché "growing pains"). How do we discern which messages are life-giving and which are soul-destroying?

Some encounters will cause harm and will not be to our benefit. We may feel doubtful about particular people or situations. Is the doubt reality knocking at our gate? Or is it an attack, mocking, "It's too late!" How do we discern the difference?

Personal Maturity: Doubt and Spiritual Attack

The enemy uses lies to shake our confidence in God. We can—and should—combat these lies in what is called *spiritual warfare.* Many experts can elaborate on the subject of spiritual warfare. My frame of reference is limited to my own experience, my reading of the experts and some excellent pastoral care. The key to discerning the religious spirit is to recognize the difference between conviction and condemnation, for we battle against flesh, the world and the devil. We want to grow and therefore welcome conviction.

Conviction

When the Holy Spirit gently and persistently leads us to recognize a flaw in our action or character, this is conviction. So, how do we deal with a critical comment from someone else when it hurts? How do we work out whether it is constructive criticism that is valid or just a nasty, unkind comment that is unworthy?

Conviction is correction—when confronted, deep down I identify the aptness of the criticism. When I'm honest with myself, I know it is a just comment. Conviction causes me to *prick up my ears*. It touches my spirit in a way that encourages me to change. When I allow myself time to be still with God to ask how to address it, He leads me *"into paths of righteousness"* and *"restores my soul."*[168] "The sorrow that is according to the will of God produces repentance without regret, leading to salvation."[169] In this context *salvation* means deliverance.

Even outside of a relationship with the Lord, our conscience can be pricked, and as part of our humanity we are frequently reminded to take responsibility for specific situations. Conviction "gnaws" at our conscience. It doesn't tear us down but pursues us quietly and persistently. Whenever I have listened to a prompting from God, I have found relief and joy from my act of repentance or apology. Unfortunately, if we ignore our conscience, eventually

---

[168] *He makes me to lie down in green pastures; He leads me beside the still waters. He restores my soul; He leads me in the paths of righteousness For His name's sake* (Psalm 23:2-3).

[169] Chuck Swindoll, *Wisdom for the Way* (Nashville, TN: Countryman, 2001), 253; see also 2 Corinthians 7:10.

the niggling feeling will fall away into silence, and an opportunity for release and growth will be lost.

If I am defensive or over-confident, haughty, proud or terribly fearful of man, when someone appears to make a critical comment, I will miss the message and the opportunity to mature. When mistaking a gentle but persistent conviction as negative criticism or condemnation, I may seem to be self-protective, but I am also self-righteous. To help discern the difference between conviction and condemnation, a friend described conviction thus: "First, God whispers to you; then He speaks a little louder. Next He taps you on the shoulder. Then He throws a brick at you!"

By considering the source and the essence of a comment directed to us, rather than ignoring it, we can work out whether it is unjust or just criticism. This process is that proverbial looking at the log in our own eye. As we consider whether it is valid or not and trust in God's sovereignty, He is able to ensure that *"all things work together for good to those who love God, to those who are the called according to His purpose."*[170] Any circumstance, however uncomfortable or hurtful, offers an opportunity for personal growth. We're all on a "learning curve," and there are probably grains of truth that we can address in whatever is said to us. Though our enemies seek to destroy us, they also are best able to see our faults, faults that are useful tools for instruction.

"But I say to you, love your enemies, bless those who curse you, do good to those who hate you, and pray for those who spitefully use you and persecute you, that you may be sons of your Father in heaven."[171] Even if what is said is erroneous or condemning, remember that when you pray for those who *"spitefully use you,"* their hearts may be won over to Jesus. Not only is this healing to

---

[170] Romans 8:28.

[171] Matthew 5:44-45a.

you, but it also miraculously restores or improves your human relationships. It certainly defeats both a cruel intention that may exist toward you and the religious spirit that provoked the criticism. When we keep a pure attitude, we will not be pulled down by others' bitterness or negativity, hurtfulness or destructive comments.

Condemnation

Now, I do not offer license to our enemies—spiritual or natural—to say or to do as they will as a means to help us to grow. Condemnation produces a feeling of shame, and that is unacceptable. Condemning words, instead of holding one's behaviour under scrutiny, actually attack the very essence of the person. If those words become embedded into our minds, a huge cloud surrounds us. In my experience, I have felt condemnation when someone has said, "A lot of people say…" with a criticism following. A way to battle the criticism without arguing with the individual is to find out who said what. If that information is not forthcoming, dismiss the comment entirely. If a negative word is not given directly, it has no validity. Often, in reality, the *people* referred to turns out to be one person without authority to comment.

If you have had your confidence, joy and identity stripped from you, you are probably experiencing condemnation. Condemnation is the opposite of grace. It does not have to be accepted. Condemnation has the power to impact us deeply and in a most cruel and ungodly way. We do it to ourselves and to others, and the devil takes great delight in causing confusion within and between us. We already know that there is no condemnation to those who are in Christ Jesus, who are called according to His purpose. So even if you feel plowed under, dug up and twisted around emotionally or mentally, you can bet that God allows it for good.

Condemnation is destructive, and its ultimate desire is death. But God in His power has already provided the opportunity for deliverance:

> "For the LORD will pass through to strike the Egyptians; and when He sees the blood on the lintel and on the two doorposts, the LORD will pass over the door and not allow the destroyer to come into your houses to strike you."[172]

If Under Condemnation

What protects us from "the death blow" of condemnation is the blood of the lamb, Jesus. With faith in Him we will not lose our joy or our rescue. And by applying Jesus' word to a situation, we can overcome.

Anyone who has suffered condemnation will know that it is a weight on the soul that stifles breath or creates a feeling of drowning. At its most profound this is spiritual attack and affects the mind by causing confusion, depression, and a sense of futility. It is not life-giving, and it is not of God. It can cause us to question ourselves, our motives, and even our faith. Unlike conviction, which seeks to draw us to God and to holiness, condemnation is despair, which in its hopelessness draws us away from God. It speaks to the soul, telling us we are a failure; it discourages us, telling us it is pointless to aspire to goodness or holiness. Whereas conviction offers hope to change, condemnation brings with it a strong sense of futility. Our spirit seems robbed of its joy, provoking us to consider death as an escape from the pain. It is completely built on lies by a devil that is the father of lies. "Hope deferred makes the heart sick"[173]; condemnation seeks to rob us of hope.

---

172 Exodus 12:23.

173 Proverbs 13:12.

Subject to Interpretation

One cautionary note about identifying condemnation: sometimes we can receive an innocent comment from someone else and take it away as something condemning. It is important to note, particularly in the healing process, that we may have a lot of baggage that affects how we interpret experiences or words. For example, I remember a particular time as an adult when I felt under scrutiny from a colleague. One day I smiled at her in passing, but she didn't smile back. I felt hurt and embarrassed and shrank away from her for weeks.

Some weeks passed, and at an awards banquet I received an award that had been initiated by the same woman I thought had judged me. At that point I realized that when she had neglected to return my smile, I had felt the same hurt I'd felt countless times as a bullied child in school. Next, I surmised that her failure to smile had probably been an oversight. When I made the connection between my feelings as an adult and the rejection I'd experienced in childhood, I realized that there must have been many times as an adult when I had felt rejected although people had probably not intended it at all. The life-changing lesson I learned from that experience was to gauge new experiences in the light of the "here and now" and not on painful experiences of the past.

Opposing Condemnation

I have encouraged you to embrace conviction as an opportunity to be set free from bad habits and imperfections. When it comes to facing condemnation, I would urge only one thing: if something is truly bothering you or hurting you, confront the person who is causing the pain and tell him or her. I would not urge you to go in fear or in anger, but when you feel confident, know that you are righteous in how you feel, and without launching a counterattack (assaulting the other person as they've assaulted you), explain that their behaviour or words have made you uncomfortable and ask them to stop the behaviour or to explain their words. This can build a bridge in your relationship with each other. In most cases people will apologize or show regret. If they deny it, it may be because they were unaware or it was unintentional. Or they may be lying. In any case, you know you have done what you can to restore your relationship. Don't go to them with a sense of expectancy but because you need to address something that has hurt you. In addressing it you will overcome the pain.

Maturity Within the Church Body: Religious Spirit Revisited

The principal entity used to attack or condemn is the religious spirit. It does not discriminate and attacks those both within and external to the church. Though as believers, Christians want to grow more like Jesus, churches quite often inadvertently create the least loving and accepting of environments. How many of us have heard "I would follow Jesus if it weren't for the Christians"?

The religious spirit is convinced that it has the right way of doing, being and thinking. Ironically, it is nothing close to representing God's image of love. It works on the principle of shame, and it cringes at freedom. If a person is too full of life or too different, it attempts to shame him into behaving as he "should" according to the specific code that equates all behaviour to its lowest common denominator. This is not of God. His Spirit desires us to worship in spirit and in truth, in the freedom Jesus died to give to us. The religious spirit is confused; it equates *should* with the righteousness of God and *uniformity* with the unity of the spirit. One day the entire church will be free from this ungodly spirit, and we can look forward to that day. In the meantime, we must recognize and pray against its pressure, pray that everyone comes out from under it, and forgive those who say or do hurtful things as unwitting accomplices to it.

Exhortation and Edification

Exhortation and edification are gifts God has given to us to build up and make more accountable the children of God and society as a whole. Edification is what is spoken regarding the successes, righteousness and wholeness within a group or an individual. Exhortation is the flipside, the means by which God speaks to us of our shortcomings.

One clear biblical example of exhortation is found in Revelation 2–3, where He tells the seven churches their strengths, then their weaknesses, in an effort to build them from where they are to where they can be.

Oppression is opposite to the encouraging twins edification and exhortation. It seeks to control, and it stifles freedom. It comes in the name of "order." Unfortunately, the church has been a key player used to exercise oppression in society. "Fire and brimstone" preaching condemned whole societies and put fear into the hearts of churchgoers. But in offering the threat of death without the available promise of light and life through faith alone, there is hopelessness. The gospel needs to be preached alongside the consequences of sin.

Conversely, as an over-reaction to that history, today many leaders who accept the prophetic move of God encourage edification but discourage exhortation. As one gifted in exhortation, I have been sensitive to the fact that words of exhortation are nervously received.

Leadership

Leaders have a tough job, and a good pastor wants to protect his flock from injury while still encouraging it to grow. It is not an easy or enviable task. Church leaders, and managers in the secular world, need our prayers of encouragement and our support.

Rebuke

The opposite to a religious spirit of criticism is rebuke, which is transparent. Although it may be unpleasant to hear a rebuke, it is by its nature clear, direct and outspoken and actually bears the fruit of truth, light, beauty, grace and love. While rebuke is criticism, it arises from the objective observation of a genuine error and seeks to address that error as a means to teach and encourage a biblical lifestyle. It is not subjective but is based on biblical principles of godly behaviour. Most importantly, it is offered in love.

From time to time each of us is called to account for our behaviour. The Spirit of God works to cleanse through rebuke, exhortation and edification, and always in grace and love.

Experiencing the Condemnation of the Religious Spirit

It is fundamental in our spiritual and emotional growth to understand that we are subject to God's scrutiny and that it is healthful. But it is also crucial to recognize the imitator of God's conviction: the religious spirit. Personal experience inside and outside of the church has taught me to identify the religious spirit. God has strengthened me by allowing me to be exposed to the power of the religious spirit. It has had its negative impact upon me so that I could learn how to overcome my shame. The condemnation I have faced and learned to overcome is "the silent treatment." I faced its crippling power of silence on two particular occasions. Uncertain whether I was imagining rejection or if in fact the rejection was real, I could not be certain without being verbally confronted. At first I felt dismayed, not knowing even if the rejection existed outside of my own imagination. Uncertainty was the gateway for confusion, fear, self-condemnation, utter loneliness and misery.

181

The first experience was within dysfunctional family relationships. One spring day many years ago I went to visit family members for a birthday party. What was planned to be a celebration would be the termination of relationship. It had been decided among the family, without my knowledge, that I was to be cast out of the circle unless I recanted an unpopular truth I had spoken.

I arrived at the party and felt that the air was thick with tension. I felt nauseous. But each person carried on as though there was no tension. I felt cold stares but was not confronted. In spite of the superficial chatter, I felt the tension and became increasingly ill. Partway through dinner I finally said I felt really sick to my stomach and would need to leave promptly. I had a ten-mile country drive to get home, and I was unsure I'd be physically able to manage it.

The immediate result was an outburst of condemnation: I was selfish, I was seeking attention, and I was faking illness in order to get out of having to be there.

I'd never before, nor have I since, felt physically ill from condemnation, but upon reflection, the religious spirit was at work in those family members as they bade me to conform, to lie in order to keep the family in comfortable denial, or never to show my face again—all this without a word being spoken about it.

Finally, as I was leaving, my mother blurted out the true issue at hand: that I was unwelcome as a part of the family until or unless I retracted what I'd said to one member privately a few days before. (Eventually the relationship with my mother was partly restored, though not the relationship with the others.) Although the pain and rejection from my family took time to resolve within myself, I am now free from the condemnation I experienced and stronger for having had to overcome it. I find I am better equipped to encourage others through similar struggles. It also prepared me to face the religious spirit's power over godly men in a Spirit-filled church.

Three thousand miles from the first experience and fifteen years later, I experienced the "silent treatment" again, as a tool of discouragement. I would say that the enemy of God may work in our lives in a particular way as long as it is effective. Once we come up against and learn to repel and overcome its destructive force, it loses its authority and effectiveness.

I take you back to a story I told earlier about singing in church at a healing meeting. In my zeal to worship the Lord and to bless others, I sang an improvised song. My motive was to bless, but in the eyes of a leader in the church, I had stepped out of place and had drawn attention to myself. Through the silence I received from the leader, the condemnation was clear. I had held this leader in such high regard, so I became disillusioned and speechless.

Putting these two experiences together, after a fruitful quest with God for clarity, I realized the enemy's strategy: silence and polite unspoken rejection was an effective way to oppress and control me. By seeing the enemy's strategy I was able to overcome it at last. Now I speak directly into that silence or rejection by sowing love and prompting communication as the gateway for relationship.

Who Is Most Vulnerable to the Religious Spirit?

How does the religious spirit get a foothold, and how can we ensure its defeat?

The religious spirit operates in and through those who believe themselves superior, who condescend to help or teach others, who in effect are self-righteous. Anyone who does not remain truly humble and open to constructive criticism is himself vulnerable to it. Leaders take protection! Those who are called to shepherd must remember Paul's words in Romans chapter 1: "*For I long to see you, that I may impart to you some spiritual gift to*

*strengthen you, that is, **that we may be mutually encouraged by
each other's faith, both yours and mine**"* (Romans 1:11–12, RSV,
emphasis added).*

While he was teaching, writing to those less mature in Christ or
less knowledgeable of God's heart, Paul nevertheless equated himself
with them. The relationship built each of them, passing benefit not
only from him to them but in reciprocity. This learned and gifted
man, who spoke in humility to those less experienced or mature, is an
example to all in leadership today.

Defeating the Religious Spirit

We will defeat the religious spirit by recognizing it, refusing to
bow to it, and instead, using prayer, to attack it. This spirit can take
years to overcome…or only a moment. It requires faith, patience and
persistence. Above all, it takes grace to not attack the persons through
whom it may be operating. Loving them in spite of their attitude can
be the tool God uses to open their eyes to their error. In any case, if
we are committed to Him this is a requirement of His, and we are to
walk in obedience as we surrender to Him.[174]

The power of Scripture plus faith will conquer this controlling spirit. Warfare begins by applying God's tools, as highlighted
in Ephesians 6:10–18,[175] through prayer. The armour of God is

---

* See also Ezekiel 34—the chapter rebukes leaders who have not taken
care of the people. This culminates in verse 10: *Thus says the Lord GOD:
"Behold, I **am** against the shepherds, and I will require My flock at their
hand; I will cause them to cease feeding the sheep, and the shepherds shall feed
themselves no more; for I will deliver My flock from their mouths, that they
may no longer be food for them."*

[174] *"This is My commandment, that you love one another as I have loved
you"* (John 15:12).

[175] *Finally, my brethren, be strong in the Lord and in the power of His might.
Put on the whole armor of God, that you may be able to stand against…*

predominantly defensive. Our offensive weapon is the Word of God, which may be applied through prayer alone.

This book is not designed to teach God's Word or spiritual warfare, but as you make the effort to learn, you will have the armour you need to conquer the enemy. The enemy is not people but, as it says in Ephesians 6, powers and principalities and rulers of this present darkness. This is hard work, but many can testify that it is well worth the effort.

To the unbeliever I can best offer the hope of salvation to conquer this spirit. I believe it is this evil religious spirit that drove the God-fearing Vincent Van Gogh to madness and Jerry Lee Lewis to rebellion and that it seeks to crush creativity and spontaneity. I believe it drives many to sin as an overreaction to its pressure.

When the religious spirit is overcome and defeated rather than indulged, there is true freedom and a release into one's identity in Christ. There will be a fresh determination to be who we were created to be, without a need to prove anything to anybody. This determination is a sense of setting one's face like flint to the purposes of God and of holding fast to the confidence of God.[176]

---

*...the wiles of the devil. For we do not wrestle against flesh and blood, but against principalities, against powers, against the rulers of the darkness of this age, against spiritual **hosts** of wickedness in the heavenly **places**. Therefore take up the whole armor of God, that you may be able to withstand in the evil day, and having done all, to stand. Stand therefore, having girded your waist with truth, having put on the breastplate of righteousness, and having shod your feet with the preparation of the gospel of peace; above all, taking the shield of faith with which you will be able to quench all the fiery darts of the wicked one. And take the helmet of salvation, and the sword of the Spirit, which is the word of God; praying always with all prayer and supplication in the Spirit, being watchful to this end with all perseverance and supplication for all the saints* (Ephesians 6:10-18).

[176] *But Christ as a Son over His own house, whose house we are if we hold fast the confidence and the rejoicing of the hope firm to the end* (Hebrews 3:6).

"To him that overcometh will I grant to sit with me in my throne, even as I also overcame, and am set down with my Father in his throne."[177] This is the greatest reward.

Summary

Conviction comes from the Holy Spirit and draws us to repentance. It is life-giving. Condemnation is the opposite in every way, damning us and pulling us away from hope and joy and God.

All criticism needs to be weighed and considered, even if later discarded. We can learn and grow even from considering our adversary's perspective.

The religious spirit is a primary mechanism through which condemnation thrives. It seeks to oppress that which is different from itself. The religious spirit, though having nothing to do with God, operates in church settings as well as outside of them.

Today churches often recognize edification but more rarely exhortation, which is a godly way of checking the behaviour or attitude of a believer. Instead, sadly, some churches still operate with a religious spirit, which is the ungodly pressure to control behaviour and attitude.

Oppression is a spirit, which also seeks to control behaviour. It stifles freedom by causing us to be heavy-hearted, timid or too frightened to step out of line for fear of rejection, condemnation or segregation.

The religious spirit operates through those who lack humility toward others. The religious spirit can be overcome through prayer and the use of God's Word. For this we also need faith.

---

[177] Revelation 3:21, KJV.

True freedom comes when we defeat condemnation through the power of the Holy Spirit.

Scriptures

*And we know that all things work together for good to those who love God, to those who are the called according to **His** purpose* (Romans 8:28).

*"No weapon formed against you shall prosper, And every tongue **which** rises against you in judgment You shall condemn. This **is** the heritage of the servants of the LORD, and their righteousness **is** from Me," Says the LORD* (Isaiah 54:17).

*For the weapons of our warfare **are** not carnal but mighty in God for pulling down strongholds* (2 Corinthians 10:4).

Chapter 14

Ignoring Anxiety, Living in Freedom

Finally, it is possible to overcome anxiety simply by choice, because whatever attitude we hold toward any situation is ultimately our choice.

My spouse once taught me how to hold thoughts captive: to take a negative thought—a worry or anxiety—and mentally to peg it down and walk away from it, refusing to let the thought hold me captive. Ignoring anxiety is not actually a mental exercise, the will or soul meditating on emptiness or learning to deny or avoid discomfort. It is not "mind over matter," seeking to find inner peace and spiritual calm through yoga or meditation. Rather, it is choosing to not dwell on negative possibilities; it is allowing the gift of joy we receive from the Holy Spirit to lift us out of our circumstances.

What Is Our Attitude?

Psychologist Kevin Higgins says, "Our response to suffering shapes our character and determines our psychological and spiritual health."[178] Victor Frankl, a Viennese psychiatrist sent to a concentration camp during WWII, told of his reaction to guards

---

[178] Kevin Higgins, quoted in Selwyn Hughes, *Every Day with Jesus* (Jan/Feb 2004), Wednesday, February 4.

who stripped him of his jewellery: "You can rob me of my belong-
ings but you cannot rob me of my choice to respond to what you
are doing to me."[179] He chose not to hate, knowing that would
poison his entire personality. Instead, he used the situation as a
study, and he'd use his conclusions as professional research should
he survive the war.[180] By finding purpose in his situation, he did
not break.

Worship Is Another Key

When we are low, if we look upward in worship, we will be
made free. To worship we focus on Jesus; to focus on Jesus takes
attention off ourselves. We are relieved of stress, doubt and anxiety;
we forget. *"If a man should live many years, let him rejoice in them
all."*[181] So, let us rejoice and enjoy God now.

> A catechism in the Presbyterian Church begins with the
> question, "what is the chief end of man?" The answer to
> that question is familiar to many: "The chief end of man
> is to love God and enjoy Him forever." Not just serve
> Him, not just obey Him, not just sacrifice to Him, not
> simply commit ourselves to Him, but enjoy Him—"laugh
> through life with Him." Smile in His presence. So much
> more is included in enjoying Him forever than most
> would ever believe.[182]

To worship God in spirit and in truth ensures boundless joy
and freedom.

---

[179] Victor Frankl, quoted in Hughes, *Every Day with Jesus.*

[180] Hughes, *Every Day with Jesus.*

[181] Ecclesiastes 11:8, New American Standard Bible.

[182] Swindoll, *Wisdom for the Way,* 245.

Reading God's Word

The third and final means to overcoming the habit of living in anxiety is to read the Bible.

How many of us, when feeling low, are tempted to "comfort eat" or to read a novel or watch television in order to offer ourselves temporary relief and distraction from worrisome thoughts? It is so much more powerful to read the Word of God, which distracts *and heals* as well. Let's test ourselves: when we finish reading the Word, aren't we in a different—a much calmer and more peaceful—place than when we started? Our whole perspective on a problem will have changed; that is superior to the brief respite offered by food or entertainment. Even reading passages that we do not understand can supernaturally bring comfort and healing in our area of distress. The Holy Spirit is in the Book, Jesus is the Word of the Book, and in spending time considering God's Word, there is a healing process available like no other.

This is not to suggest that medical attention is never required for the treatment of a physical or psychological ailment. But the supernatural power of God can bring restoration directly or can work in co-operation with medicine to hasten or deepen the healing process.

What Is Our Mindset?

The root to anxiety and the overcoming of it is in the power of our mind. The mind—or soul, as it is referred to in Judeo-Christian tradition—is the sum of our will, intellect and emotion. Psychologists have proven that our thoughts trigger our emotions, and our will can override both when we choose the attitudes we will hold toward any given circumstance. As we surrender our will to our (living) spirit, and our spirit to the Holy Spirit, He will override our mind and give us victory through His Spirit over our flesh, the world and the enemy Satan. Unlike with soulful meditation, we do not attempt to conquer anxiety. Rather, God's Spirit rescues us like no one else can. "*Now to him who by the power at work within us is able to do far more abundantly than all that we ask or think, to him be glory.*"[183] Victory over flesh is by the Spirit.

It Is a Choice to Be Healed

Ultimately, to carry an attitude of acceptance or bitterness is our own choice. A worshipful attitude will put our focus on the Source of power and away from ourselves. Our mind is the weaker entity, and in accepting His power we hold a key to overcoming worry. Reading the Bible and developing our understanding of Scripture also gives us power to rise above anxiety.

My personal philosophy is that we will never succeed in overcoming insecurity so long as we focus on ourselves. To focus on "me" is a form of madness. To the degree that we do not think like Jesus Christ, the wisest teacher, greatest physician, most noble philanthropist to ever walk the earth, to that degree I believe we are less than fully rational and not completely right in our minds. Truth, beauty, loveliness—therein lays sanity. Thinking pure, good thoughts enables our minds to be refreshed and at peace.

"*Finally, brethren, whatever is true, whatever is honorable, whatever is just, whatever is pure, whatever is lovely, whatever is gracious, if there is any excellence, if there is anything worthy of praise, think about these things.*"[184] As we live lives of worship, we delight the Lord. As we receive our delight from Him, we are best able to see His purposes and to step into His destiny and calling for our lives. Joy, peace, love, truth, purpose: all come from God and are realized as we overcome our fears and place our confidence in Him. Because

---

[183] Ephesians 3:20, RSV.

[184] Philippians 4:8, RSV.

we are called to love (and because it is best for us to be loving), our freedom is not absolute but rather exists in the context of our call to love. Paul stated in Romans,

> *And having been set free from sin, you became slaves of righteousness. I speak in human **terms** because of the weakness of your flesh. For just as you presented your members as slaves of uncleanness, and of lawlessness **leading** to **more** lawlessness, so now present your members as slaves of righteousness for holiness.*[185]

So I advocate love: to receive it from God gives us power, and to pour it out to others releases that power to make the world a more loving and secure place to live. Receive His love, deliver His love, and wholeness is inevitable.

God bless you.

Summary

We have a choice as to what thoughts we dwell on.

Worship draws us out of despair and into joy.

Reading the Bible nourishes and heals.

Freedom from fear means freedom to live in God's purposes.

Be loved, share love, and make love a priority.

Scriptures

> *Your word **is** a lamp to my feet And a light to my* path (Psalm 119:105).

> *Make a joyful noise to the LORD, all the lands! Serve the LORD with gladness! Come into his presence with singing!*

---

[185] Romans 6:18–19.

Know that the LORD is God! It is he that made us, and we are his; we are his people, and the sheep of his pasture. Enter his gates with thanksgiving, and his courts with praise! Give thanks to him, bless his name! For the LORD is good; his steadfast love endures for ever, and his faithfulness to all generations (Psalm 100:1–5, RSV).

Summary of Part V

Conviction is life-giving. It encourages change and ultimately enhances joy, but condemnation produces hopelessness, despair and emotional death. Maintaining security begins with forgiving ourselves just as we have forgiven others. Those who are able to receive constructive criticism while discerning and overcoming condemnation learn to walk in gracious humility. A truly humble heart is impervious to insecurity and low self-esteem. To be loved by God, to give love away, makes the world a more loving place.

Postscript

My mother died of cancer three years ago. I was living abroad, and I went to visit her before her death. We had been in and out of relationship for years. But I went, in spite of the fact that she said she didn't want me to go. I'm glad I went. Privately, I prayed for her healing, first emotionally—that she might have forgiveness toward me and have true reconciliation with me, because I could see that unforgiveness was eating away at her. Second, I prayed for spiritual healing, for reconciliation with God, her Maker. Third, I prayed for physical healing, which for me was the easiest prayer to have faith for. Some would think that would take a miracle, but the true miracle would be the healing from within her mind and heart.

I was nervous, even scared, to go to see my mother, because she didn't want me there. Yet, I went, because it was important, it was right, and it was necessary. There is nothing we can't face when we have the assurance and security and hope in our relationship with our Maker. Security is inside of us when we live in the grace and hope of God. In spite of her rejection I felt safe and grounded and secure sitting with her, because of my relationship with my Father in Heaven.

I loved my mother. But in seeing her, and in seeing the depth of her bitterness, I learned much about our relationship and our family that in my youth I was unable to see. What I discovered during my visit with her held the key to the insecurity that engulfed me during my childhood.

I was the youngest in my family and the least gifted intellectually. There were unspoken issues and "rules" that I was oblivious to. I believe I was spared the realization of these dictates and that if I had recognized and embraced them as a child, I would have grown into a different adult.

Every family has its unspoken rules and expectations. To embrace (or not embrace) that code influences our character and personality. It's ironic that if we are oblivious to the family rules we might be protected from them, so that instead we grow more closely into the person we were created to be, with our innate identity protected. I think that is what happened to me.

I was born a sincere person though steeped in self-centredness. I never clued into or followed the family rules, which were to "protect Father, spoil Mother, so that all will be well for you." I did not conceptualize these "rules" until the last series of visits with my mother during her illness.

As a child I was oblivious to the mould designated for me. I sensed that I was not accepted for who I was but didn't know what shape to adapt myself to in order to belong. Emotionally immature—perhaps I became fully adult at age thirty-five—I was ignorant of anything that wasn't spelled out for me. Did our family actually say, "Protect Dad emotionally, because he can't cope with real need or feeling?" Certainly not. Nor did anyone dictate that "Mom is selfish and expects us to want what she wants for us." And yet, as I listened to my mother toward the end of her life say potentially life-robbing things to me, dredging up my past mistakes as a teenager, young adult and even child, with nothing good to say to counterbalance those words, I realized that this was the same critcism I'd grown up with and that I had been ignorant of those fundamental expectations from my family. Even at her deathbed, I was never going to be acceptable, because I hadn't got the code. Yet I know, too, that by "missing it" I had actually been spared a false life. Although I'd felt the pain and loneliness of family rejection as I was growing up, because I lacked insight and did not model myself to fit in I became my own person, with some limited sense of who I was genuinely created to be.

During my visit with my mother, she defended herself against any verbal attack she thought I might launch by attacking me first. I sat and observed her inner struggle as she resisted the presence and unconditional acceptance of her daughter. I attempted to reassure her with words of affirmation and love. But through observing her self-defence I discovered something telling: she believed she'd failed. In her eyes, I'd turned out badly, because I was different. And to her that meant, ultimately, that she'd failed. And in her feeling of failure, where was her self-esteem? From where had her need to mould me originate? Had she somehow attached her self-image to how I would turn out, and failing to mould me meant she had failed?

My mother passed away three months after my visit with her. That visit was the last time I spoke with her, and although I sent a couple of letters to her, she did not respond. But a few weeks after her death, I received a letter that she'd written before her death and had arranged to have sent posthumously. In that letter she was warm, sincere and hopeful; she knew these would be her last words to me, and she wanted only good for my life. I believe my greatest, deepest and most important prayer for her healing was answered.

Parental love is not guaranteed to be unconditional. I hope as a parent myself that I will love my child however—and whomever—he turns out to be. But there is one love that is definitely unconditional, that never robs us of who we are, because He made us who we are. He never seeks to destroy our personal integrity or doubts our need. Only the love of God is guaranteed to be unconditional.

> *"Come to Me, all **you** who labor and are heavy laden, and I will give you rest. Take My yoke upon you and learn from Me, for I am gentle and lowly in heart, and you will find rest for your souls. For My yoke **is** easy and My burden is light."*[186]

---

[186] Matthew 11:28–30.

Bibliography

Holy Bible, King James Version (Authorised Version). Philadelphia, PA: The National Publishing Co., 1958.

Holy Bible, New King James Version. USA: Thomas Nelson, Inc., 1979.

The Bible, Revised Standard Version. Glasgow: CollinsBible, a division of HarperCollins Publishers, 1958, 1971.

Chapman, Gary, PhD. *The Love as a Way of Life.* London: Hodder & Stoughton, 2008.

———. *The Five Love Languages of Children.* London: Northfield Publishing, 2008.

———, Ross Campbell, MD. *The Five Love Languages of Children.* Chicago: Northfield Publishers, 1997.

Fowler, H.W. and F.G. Fowler, eds. *The Concise Oxford Dictionary of Current English*, Fourth Edition. Oxford at the Clarendon Press, 1961.

Goll, Michal Ann. *Women on the Frontlines.* Shippensburg, PA: Destiny Image Publishers, Inc., 1999.

Henry, O. *"The Gift of The Magi"*, www.literaturecollection. com/a/o_henry.

Hughes, Selwyn. "Everyday With Jesus." CWR Publishers, Jan/Feb 2004 edition.

Jellis, Susan. *Encarta Thesaurus*. London: Bloomsbury Publishing, 2001.

Lewis, C.S. *The Screwtape Letters*. San Francisco: Harper, 1942.

Swindoll, Charles. Wisdom for the Way. Nashville, TN: J. Countryman, a division of Thomas Nelson Publ., 2001.

Thatcher, Virginia S., Editor in chief. *The New Webster Encyclopedic Dictionary of the English Language*. Chicago: Consolidated Book Publishers, 1971.

Watchman, Nee. *Do All to the Glory of God*. New York: Christian Fellowship Publishers, Inc., 1974.

Mental Health America, Central Virginia: www.mentalhealthamerica.net

Scripture Index

General Index

sanity and 192
set free by 94, 153, 166
telling the 15
unpopular 182
versus darkness 166
versus lie 89
versus opinion 137
walk in 146
worship 142, 179, 190

Vulnerability: 14, 37, 110, 140
others' 144

Weapon: 15, 185

Word:
affirmation 197
application 177, 186
critical 196
guard 113, 122
interpretation 178
Jesus 191
... of God (Bible) 20, 25, 33, 52, 57, 121
power 30, 32, 33, 57, 109, 176, 191
prayer using 34, 60, 94, 185

protection 69
study of 127
versus silence 182

Worship:
ancestral 62
attitude 192
culture 139
focus 190
God 59
healing 193
inspired 183
style 134, 142
team 22

Order Form for Additional Copies
of Free to Be

Please send me _____ copies

Ordered by: _____

Address: _____

City: _____ Prov./State: _____

Postal/Zip Code: _____

Email (to confirm order): _____

Telephone (optional): _____

Please allow 4 weeks for delivery

**Free to Be can be ordered by post or email. Please send
cheques or money order for $18.95
plus postage and handling to**

Sarah Tun
Box 72
Bath, Ontario
CANADA
K0H 1G0

Postage rates:

Within Canada	1 book: $4.00 each
	2 books: $11.00
To USA	1 book: $8.00 each
	2 books: $13.00
Overseas	1 book: $15.00 each
	2 books: $16.00

Contact in advance for bulk orders